Uncover 4

Combo B

Ben Goldstein • Ceri Jones
with Kathryn O'Dell

Student's Book

CAMBRIDGE
UNIVERSITY PRESS

32 Avenue of the Americas, New York, NY 10013-2473, USA

Cambridge University Press is part of the University of Cambridge.

It furthers the University's mission by disseminating knowledge in the pursuit of education, learning and research at the highest international levels of excellence.

www.cambridge.org
Information on this title: www.cambridge.org/9781107515154

© Cambridge University Press 2015

This publication is in copyright. Subject to statutory exception and to the provisions of relevant collective licensing agreements, no reproduction of any part may take place without the written permission of Cambridge University Press.

First published 2015

Printed in Mexico by Editorial Impresora Apolo, S.A. de C.V.

A catalog record for this publication is available from the British Library.

ISBN 978-1-107-49353-7 Student's Book 4
ISBN 978-1-107-49357-5 Student's Book with Online Workbook and Online Practice 4
ISBN 978-1-107-51514-7 Combo 4A
ISBN 978-1-107-51515-4 Combo 4B
ISBN 978-1-107-49367-4 Teacher's Book 4
ISBN 978-1-107-49364-3 Workbook with Online Practice 4
ISBN 978-1-107-49392-6 Presentation Plus Disc 4
ISBN 978-1-107-49386-5 Class Audio CDs 4
ISBN 978-1-107-49391-9 DVD 4

Additional resources for this publication at www.cambridge.org/uncover

Cambridge University Press has no responsibility for the persistence or accuracy of URLs for external or third-party internet websites referred to in this publication, and does not guarantee that any content on such websites is, or will remain, accurate or appropriate. Information regarding prices, travel timetables, and other factual information given in this work is correct at the time of first printing but Cambridge University Press does not guarantee the accuracy of such information thereafter.

Art direction, book design, layout services, and photo research: QBS Learning
Audio production: John Marshall Media

Acknowledgments

Many teachers, coordinators, and educators shared their opinions, their ideas, and their experience to help create *Uncover*. The authors and publisher would like to thank the following people and their schools for their help in shaping the series.

In Mexico:

María Nieves Maldonado Ortiz (Colegio Enrique Rébsamen); Héctor Guzmán Pineda (Liceo Europeo); Alfredo Salas López (Campus Universitario Siglo XXI); Rosalba Millán Martínez (IIPAC [Instituto Torres Quintero A.C.]); Alejandra Rubí Reyes Badillo (ISAS [Instituto San Angel del Sur]); José Enrique Gutiérrez Escalante (Centro Escolar Zama); Gabriela Juárez Hernández (Instituto de Estudios Básicos Amado Nervo); Patricia Morelos Alonso (Instituto Cultural Ingles, S.C.); Martha Patricia Arzate Fernández, (Colegio Valladolid); Teresa González, Eva Marina Sánchez Vega (Colegio Salesiano); María Dolores León Ramírez de Arellano, (Liceo Emperadores Aztecas); Esperanza Medina Cruz (Centro Educativo Francisco Larroyo); Nubia Nelly Martínez García (Salesiano Domingo Savio); Diana Gabriela González Benítez (Colegio Ghandi); Juan Carlos Luna Olmedo (Centro Escolar Zama); Dulce María Pascual Granados (Esc. Juan Palomo Martínez); Roberto González, Fernanda Audirac (Real Life English Center); Rocio Licea (Escuela Fundación Mier y Pesado); Diana Pombo (Great Union Institute); Jacobo Cortés Vázquez (Instituto María P. de Alvarado); Michael John Pryor (Colegio Salesiano Anáhuac Chapalita)

In Brazil:

Renata Condi de Souza (Colégio Rio Branco); Sônia Maria Bernal Leites (Colégio Rio Branco); Élcio Souza (Centro Universitário Anhaguera de São Paulo); Patricia Helena Nero (Private teacher); Célia Elisa Alves de Magalhães (Colégio Cruzeiro-Jacarepaguá); Lilia Beatriz Freitas Gussem (Escola Parque-Gávea); Sandra Maki Kuchiki (Easy Way Idiomas); Lucia Maria Abrão Pereira Lima (Colégio Santa Cruz-São Paulo); Deborah de Castro Ferroz de Lima Pinto (Mundinho Segmento); Clara Vianna Prado (Private teacher); Ligia Maria Fernandes Diniz (Escola Internacional de Alphaville); Penha Aparecida Gaspar Rodrigues (Colégio Salesiano Santa Teresinha); Silvia Castelan (Colégio Santa Catarina de Sena); Marcelo D'Elia (The Kids Club Guarulhos); Malyina Kazue Ono Leal (Colégio Bandeirantes); Nelma de Mattos Santana Alves (Private teacher); Mariana Martins Machado (Britannia Cultural); Lilian Bluvol Vaisman (Curso Oxford); Marcelle Belfort Duarte (Cultura Inglesa-Duque de Caxias); Paulo Dantas (Britannia International English); Anauã Carmo Vilhena (York Language Institute); Michele Amorim Estellita (Lemec – Lassance Modern English Course); Aida Setton (Colégio Uirapuru); Maria Lucia Zaorob (CEL-LEP); Marisa Veiga Lobato (Interlíngua Idiomas); Maria Virgínia Lebrón (Independent consultant); Maria Luiza Carmo (Colégio Guilherme Dumont Villares/CEL-LEP); Lucia Lima (Independent consultant); Malyina Kazue Ono Leal (Colégio Bandeirantes); Debora Schisler (Seven Idiomas); Helena Nagano (Cultura Inglesa); Alessandra de Campos (Alumni); Maria Lúcia Sciamarelli (Colégio Divina Providência); Catarina Kruppa (Cultura Inglesa); Roberto Costa (Freelance teacher/consultant); Patricia McKay Aronis (CEL-LEP); Claudia Beatriz Cavalieri (By the World Idiomas); Sérgio Lima (Vermont English School); Rita Miranda (IBI – [Instituto Batista de Idiomas]); Maria de Fátima Galery (Britain English School); Marlene Almeida (Teacher Trainer Consultant); Flávia Samarane (Colégio Logosófico); Maria Tereza Vianna (Greenwich Schools); Daniele Brauer (Cultura Inglesa/AMS Idiomas); Allessandra Cierno (Colégio Santa Dorotira); Helga Silva Nelken (Greenwich Schools/Colégio Edna Roriz); Regina Marta Bazzoni (Britain English School); Adriano Reis (Greenwich Schools); Vanessa Silva Freire de Andrade (Private teacher); Nilvane Guimarães (Colégio Santo Agostinho)

In Ecuador:

Santiago Proaño (Independent teacher trainer); Tania Abad (UDLA [Universidad de Las Americas]); Rosario Llerena (Colegio Isaac Newton); Paúl Viteri (Colegio Andino); Diego Maldonado (Central University); Verónica Vera (Colegio Tomás Moro); Mónica Sarauz (Colegio San Gabriel); Carolina Flores (Colegio APCH); Boris Cadena, Vinicio Reyes (Colegio Benalcázar); Deigo Ponce (Colegio Gonzaga); Byron Freire (Colegio Nuestra Señora del Rosario)

The authors and publisher would also like to thank the following contributors, script writers, and collaborators for their inspired work in creating *Uncover*:

Anna Whitcher, Janet Gokay, Kathryn O'Dell, Lynne Robertson and Dana Henricks

Unit	Vocabulary	Grammar	Listening	Conversation (Useful language)
6 It's the Little Things pp. 54–63	■ Everyday objects ■ Modifiers	■ Passive infinitive ■ Review of causative *have/get* Grammar reference p. 111	■ All kinds of unusual things	■ Buying a gadget
7 Have a Ball! pp. 64–73	■ Celebration phrases ■ Descriptive adjectives	■ verb + *-ing* form (gerund) or infinitive ■ *-ing* form (gerund) as subject ■ *by/for* + *-ing* form Grammar reference p. 112	■ Weird and wonderful celebrations	■ Making exclamations
8 Mysteries and Secrets pp. 74–83	■ Adjectives with *un-* ■ Reporting verbs	■ Time clauses ■ Present participle clauses ■ Reported speech ■ Indirect questions Grammar reference p. 113	■ A mysterious act of kindness	■ Confirming and denying
9 Weird and Wonderful pp. 84–93	■ Story elements ■ Linking phrases	■ Third conditional ■ *wish* + past perfect ■ Past modals of speculation Grammar reference p. 114	■ Who or what is a hoodoo?	■ Asking for more information
10 I Have To! I Can! pp. 94–103	■ Training and qualifications ■ Jobs	■ Past ability ■ Modal expressions for past and future ■ *make* and *let* Grammar reference p. 115	■ Job talk	■ Making decisions

Unit 6–10 Review Game pp. 104–105

Writing	Reading	Video	Accuracy and fluency	Speaking outcomes
A product review for a gadget	Light in a Bottle Reading to Write: Let's Hear It For Headphones! Culture: Before There Was Texting	Survival Objects What's your favorite gadget? The Start of the Web Inside the Guitar (CLIL Project p. 118)	get/have for actions done for someone else dropping consonant sounds with kind of	I can . . . talk about everyday objects and why they're important. talk about new uses for everyday objects. talk about inventions. talk about how inventions have changed the world.
A description of a celebration	How to Plan a Party Reading to Write: A Great Family Party! Culture: Korea: Coming of Age	Let's Celebrate What's the worst party you've ever been to? Like Father, Like Daughter	Using so and too Word stress with verb + infinitive	I can . . . talk about party preparations and activities. plan an end-of-school party. describe events and festivals. talk about coming-of-age celebrations.
A story about a secret	A Secret Under the Street Reading to Write: The Secret Room Culture: An Unbelievable Book	A Lost Civilization What's the biggest lie you've ever been told? Mysteries of the Brain Reliving History (CLIL Project p. 119)	Time clauses in present tense with future Intonation with indirect questions	I can . . . describe unusual events. talk about an imaginary discovery. solve a mystery by using reported speech and questions. discuss world mysteries.
A story about an event	Lucky's Luck Reading to Write: Bicycle Accident! Culture: Mesa Verde: Homes Up High	On the Run What's the biggest mistake you've ever made? Insectmobile	so that and in order to Shortening had and would with third conditional	I can . . . talk about the story elements in a story. talk about imaginary situations in the past. discuss possible explanations for past events. talk about what my life might have been like in the past.
A biography about a musician	Building a Dream Reading to Write: A Singing Star Culture: Young and Talented Australians	Future Directions What do you see yourself doing ten years from now? The Young and the Brave Lions in Danger (CLIL Project p. 120)	Not using could for ability in certain cases Eliding words ending in vowels with words beginning with vowels	I can . . . talk about my plans after graduation. discuss careers and abilities. talk about my abilities and obligations in the past. compare someone's abilities and obligations to mine.

rregular verbs p. 121

6 It's the Little Things

Discovery EDUCATION

BE CURIOUS

Survival Objects

What's your favorite gadget?

The Start of the Web

Inside the Guitar

1. What are the objects in the photo? What objects are they made out of?

2. Do you think it's a good idea? Why or why not?

3. Do you ever use objects for other purposes? Explain.

UNIT CONTENTS

Vocabulary Everyday objects; Modifiers
Grammar Passive infinitive; Review of causative *have/get*
Listening All kinds of unusual things

Vocabulary: Everyday objects

1. Label the pictures with the correct words.

| a candle | a fan | a light bulb | a remote control | an air conditioner |
| a charger | ✓ a heater | a plug | a switch | matches |

1. _a heater_    2.  _____   3. _____   4. _____

5. _____   6. _____   7.  _____   8. _____

9. _____   10. _____

> **NOTICE IT**
> A system that cools a house or car is sometimes called *air conditioning* instead of *an air conditioner*.
> *It's hot in the car. Can you turn on the air conditioning?*

 2. Listen, check, and repeat.

3. What are the objects in Exercise 1 used for? Complete the chart.

to provide light or to light something	_a candle_	_____	_____
to heat or cool something	_____	_____	_____
to turn something on	_____	_____	
to give electricity to something	_____	_____	

Speaking: We need it!

4. YOUR TURN Work with a partner. Discuss why the objects from Exercise 1 are important. Which three do you think are the most important?

> *A heater is important because it helps us stay warm when it's cold.*

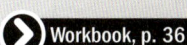 Workbook, p. 36

Reading Light in a Bottle; Let's Hear It for Headphones!; Before There Was Texting
Conversation Buying a gadget
Writing A product review for a gadget

Useful INVENTIONS

Light in a Bottle

Imagine a light bulb that doesn't need electricity or plugs and doesn't cost anything to run. Alfredo Moser invented the bottle lamp in Brazil more than 10 years ago. He was trying to help people in his hometown, which often had problems with electricity. Sometimes there was only enough electricity for the factories, and people's homes and small businesses were left in the dark. One day, Moser and his friend were talking about how a light should be created for emergencies. One of them suggested using water in a bottle to reflect the light from the sun. Moser likes to be challenged. He thought, *Why not use water to make a lamp?* It was a great way to create a lamp that didn't have to be plugged in.

His invention is very simple. Start with a clear, plastic bottle. First, fill it with water. Then add some bleach to keep the water clean and clear. Finally, the bottle needs to be closed with a black top. The black top attracts the sun. When the lamp is finished, cut a small hole in the roof and push the bottle through it. The sunlight comes in through the bottle and lights the room below. The light is much stronger than light from a candle!

Moser's lamp bottles were installed in the local supermarket. Moser was happy to help his community. He didn't expect to be known around the world for his invention, but that's just what happened. Ten years later, the MyShelter Foundation in the Philippines heard about Moser's invention. The organization helps people in poor areas and specializes in building houses with recycled materials. They use plastic bottles to make walls and windows, but they had never thought of using them to make light. Now there are Moser lamps in more than 140,000 homes throughout the Philippines. The idea has spread to several other countries, too. Moser's bottle lamps have definitely made life easier for a lot of people!

Reading: An article about an invention

1. **Look at the pictures. What is the invention? What everyday object is it made from?**

2. **Read and listen to the article. Complete the chart.**

1. Inventor	
2. Country	
3. Reason for the invention	
4. Where it was first used	
5. Where it was used 10 years later	

3. **Read the article again. Number the steps to making a bottle light.**

   ____ Make a hole in the roof.   ____ Put the bottle in the hole.

   ____ Put bleach in the water.   ____ Put the top on the bottle.

   ____ Get a plastic bottle.   ____ Put water in the bottle.

4. **YOUR TURN** Work with a partner. In what other ways can people use plastic bottles or other everyday objects?

   > You can keep rice in plastic bottles.

   > Yeah. You can use old candles to fix furniture.

DID YOU KNOW…?

In India, people use bottle lamps in schools, and they also use them to grow food in some areas. In Bangladesh, the lights are used in small businesses.

Grammar: Passive infinitive

5. Complete the chart.

Present	Past
The passive is the main verb + to be + a past participle. The main verb usually expresses thinking or speaking, for example: *be, have, know, want, need, expect, like, believe,* and *ask.*	
The bottle **needs** _____ **closed** with a black top. Moser **likes to be challenged**.	The lamp **didn't have to be plugged** in. He **didn't expect** _____ **known** around the world for his invention.

> Check your answers: Grammar reference, p. 111

6. Write sentences in the passive infinitive. Use the simple present for the main verb.

1. Brett / want / know / for his Web designs
   Brett wants to be known for his Web designs.

2. we / ask / inform / about all new projects
   _____

3. Carmela / not like / tell / what to do
   _____

4. the store lights / need / turn off / at night
   _____

5. the air conditioner / be / fix / next week
   _____

6. Lynn / expect / greet / at the inventor's workshop
   _____

7. Rewrite the sentences. Use the modals in parentheses.

1. The switch needs to be turned off. (must)
   The switch must be turned off.

2. The matches need to be dry before you can use them. (should)
   _____

3. The tablet needs to be repaired. (must)
   _____

4. Susana is to be picked up after school. (had better)
   _____

5. The new smartphone is expected to be sold in the fall. (might)
   _____

> The passive with a modal can sometimes be used to convey a similar meaning to a passive infinitive sentence.
>
> The bottle **needs to be closed** with a black top. →
> The bottle **must be closed** with a black top.
>
> To form the passive with modals, use modal + be + past participle.
>
> A light **should be created** for emergencies.

Speaking: More inventions

8. YOUR TURN Work with a partner. Think of three inventions for each category. Which invention is the most useful in each category?

1. Things that need to be plugged in
2. Things that don't need to be plugged in
3. Things that could be used at school and at home
4. Things that should be repaired regularly

> Computers need to be plugged in.
>> Yeah. And smartphones need to be plugged in.

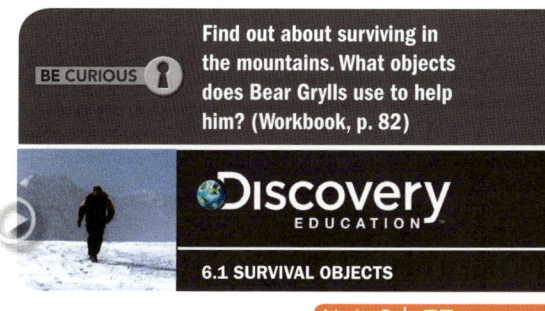

Find out about surviving in the mountains. What objects does Bear Grylls use to help him? (Workbook, p. 82)

6.1 SURVIVAL OBJECTS

Buying and FIXING

Listening: All kinds of unusual things

1. Have you ever shopped at a market? What did they sell? Did you buy anything?

2. Listen to a man looking for a cheap, useful object at a market. Number the objects in the order he talks about them. Which object does he buy?

   _____ a. solar charger
   _____ b. handheld fan
   _____ c. floor lamp/heater

3. Listen again. Match the objects (a–c) to the sentences (1–6).

   1. These objects are expensive. _____ _____
   2. This object does two different things. _____
   3. This object is available in different colors. _____
   4. This object is available in different styles. _____
   5. This object can be sent to your house. _____
   6. This object uses sunlight. _____

NOTICE IT
Kind of has two meanings:
A modifier that means *fairly*: My smartphone is **kind of** small.
A phrase that means *a type/sort*: The AL20 is a **kind of** smartphone.

Vocabulary: Modifiers

4. Read the sentences and check (✓) the correct column. Then listen and check your answers.

	–	+
1. This charger is **kind of** big. I'd rather have a smaller one.		✓
2. The light bulb is **extremely** bright. It will be great for reading.		
3. That lamp is **ridiculously** expensive. It's $1,000!		
4. That invention is **not really** useful. I don't think anyone will buy it.		
5. That fan is **totally** safe. There's no way you could cut your finger on it.		
6. That air conditioner is **so** old. I don't even think it works anymore.		
7. That case is **a little bit** small for my phone. It doesn't quite fit.		
8. That heater is **far too** pricey. We can find a much cheaper one online.		

5. **YOUR TURN** Work with a partner. Talk about the items that you have. Use the adjectives below and modifiers from Exercise 4.

Item	Adjectives
phone	small, expensive
tablet or computer	big, new
bicycle	pricey, light
desk	old, heavy

> My phone is extremely small. It was kind of expensive.

> Really? My phone wasn't really expensive. It...

Say it RIGHT!

The phrase **kind of** often sounds like *kind-a*. However, when the following word starts with a vowel, the *f* is usually pronounced. Listen to the sentences.
My phone was **kind of** small.
My phone was **kind of** expensive.
Pay attention to the way you pronounce **kind of** in Exercise 5.

Grammar: Review of causative have/get

6. Complete the chart.

> Use causative have/get in situations where someone else does something for you or when it's not important who is doing the action. You can use have or get. They have similar meanings.
> Use have/get + an object + past participle with the present, past, and future.

	Active	Passive/Causative
Simple present	Someone **cleans** her house on Thursdays.	She **has** her house **cleaned** on Thursdays.
Simple past	Someone **delivered** the lamp today.	We **got** the lamp **delivered** today.
Present continuous	No one **is sending** the lamp to the man's house.	The man **isn't having** a lamp _____ to his house.
Future with will	I **will ask** someone **to make** a designer battery charger for my sister.	I **will get** a designer battery charger _____ for my sister.
Modals	**Should** I **ask** someone **to wrap** them for you?	Should I **have** them _____ for you?

> Check your answers: Grammar reference, p. 111

7. Look at Sandra's calendar. Write sentences about her activities.

Monday	Tuesday	Wednesday	Thursday	Friday
get / clothes / clean	have / car heater / check	*Today – Now* get / hair / do	get / computer / upgrade	get / camera / fix

1. On Monday, Sandra got her clothes cleaned_____.
2. On Tuesday, she _____.
3. Today, _____.
4. Tomorrow, _____.
5. On Friday, _____.

8. Rewrite the sentences. Change the active to passive.

1. Someone painted our nails at the new salon. (get) We got our nails painted at the new salon.
2. Someone will fix Laurie's bike next week. (have) _____
3. Someone won't fix my phone until next week. (have) _____
4. Someone is repairing Sam's skateboard. (get) _____
5. Someone was painting your house last week. (have) _____
6. Someone had stolen Marta's purse at the mall. (get) _____

Speaking: It's broken!

9. YOUR TURN Write notes about problems you had with objects that you couldn't fix yourself.

My tablet crashed, my bicycle broke, . . .

10. Work with a partner. Talk about the problems from Exercise 9 and what you got/had done about them.

> My tablet crashed last week. I had it fixed right away. The computer technician got it done in one day!

> My bicycle broke. I didn't get it fixed yet, but my sister will try to fix it tomorrow.

> **Get it RIGHT!**
> Use **get**, not **have**, when the subject is doing the action for someone else. The computer technician fixed the tablet. She **got** it **done** for me in one day. (NOT: She **had** it **done** for me in one day.)

REAL TALK 6.2 WHAT'S YOUR FAVORITE GADGET?

Gadgets are GOOD!

Conversation: Getting gadgets

1. **REAL TALK** Watch or listen to the teenagers talk about their favorite gadgets. Check (✓) their favorite items.

   ☐ an alarm clock ☐ a desk lamp ☐ a phone ☐ a stress ball
   ☐ a camera ☐ a flashlight ☐ a reading light ☐ a tablet

2. **YOUR TURN** What's *your* favorite gadget? Tell your partner.

3. Eddie is shopping for a new phone. Listen and complete the conversation with the words in the box.

USEFUL LANGUAGE: Buying a gadget

✓ Could you show me | How good is | Is it . . . to use? | Does it have | How long does | Which mo[del]

Eddie: Excuse me. ¹ _Could you show me_ some of your smartphones?
Clerk: Sure. Did you have one in mind?
Eddie: Not really. ² _____ the best?
Clerk: I like this one – the TS500.
Eddie: OK. ³ _____ easy _____
Clerk: Oh, yes. It's extremely user-friendly.
Eddie: Great. And ⁴ _____ the battery last?
Clerk: About 8 hours.
Eddie: That's not bad. ⁵ _____ the sound?
Clerk: It's pretty good.
Eddie: I see. And can I put a lot of songs on it? How much memory does it have?
Clerk: You can download thousands of songs. You can get it with 16G, 32G, or 64G of memory.
Eddie: OK. I need 32G. ⁶ _____ a camera?
Clerk: Of course! Anything else?
Eddie: Oh, yeah. How much does it cost?
Clerk: For the 32G? $150.
Eddie: Hmm . . . that's a little bit pricey, but I'll take it.

NOTICE IT
The **G** in **16G** means gigabytes. It is often pronounced as "gig" or "gigs."

4. Practice the conversation with a partner.

5. **YOUR TURN** Work with a partner. Take turns asking a clerk about a gadget. Use one of the items below or your own ideas.

Gadget	A tablet	An e-reader
Model	Storm5000	Etric6
Battery life	10 hours	20 hours
Sound quality	extremely good	not really good
Memory	64G or 128G	8G or 16G
Camera	yes	no
Price	64G = $350 128G = $450	8G = $75 16G = $125

60 | Unit 6

★★★★☆ **HEADPHONES!**

posted by Ji Ah Rhee on January 6, 2015

I bought the Magicmusic G42 Headphones at magicmusic.com for $39.99.

The design is modern, and they are available in black and red. The headphones have a noise-canceling switch. It doesn't need to be turned on, but when it's on, you hear only your music, not the noise in the room. While most headphones have short cords, these have an extremely long one. They also come with a travel case that's kind of cool.

The sound quality is ridiculously good! It sounds like your favorite bands are right in front of you. The headphone volume goes from quiet to extremely loud. One problem: The headphones arrived broken! I had the package sent back, and the company did replace the headphones right away.

These headphones are a great value for the money. Whereas other headphones have stopped working after a few months, these headphones are lasting a long time. I've been totally happy with them and recommend them to other music lovers.

Reading to write: A product review for a gadget

6. Look at the photo, title, and number of stars. What did Ji Ah buy? Did she like it? Read her product review to check.

   ○ *Focus on* **CONTENT**
   When you write a product review for a gadget, include these things:
   - the name of the product, price, and where you bought it
   - the design and features
   - the quality (what works and what doesn't)
   - your opinion of the product and recommendation

7. Read Ji Ah's product review again. What information did she give for each item in the Focus on Content box?

   ○ *Focus on* **LANGUAGE**
   Use *while* and *whereas* to compare one product to another. They have the same meaning.
   While the older model only has 32G of memory, the new model has 128G.
   The new model has 128G of memory, **while** the older model only has 32G.

   Whereas a tablet has a short battery life, an e-reader has a long one.
   An e-reader has a long battery life, **whereas** a tablet has a short one.

8. Find the sentences in Ji Ah's product review with *while* and *whereas*.

9. Are *while* and *whereas* used correctly? Write **Y** (yes) or **N** (no).
   1. The lamp has a light bulb, whereas it's also a heater. __N__
   2. While most battery chargers are far too big, this one is extremely small. ____
   3. The new air conditioner has 10 cooling settings, whereas the old model only had five. ____
   4. While energy-efficient light bulbs use less electricity, so I bought some. ____
   5. Whereas a typical fan has to be plugged in, this one is cordless. ____
   6. Candles are useful in a storm, while your flashlight has to have batteries. ____

Writing: Your product review for a gadget

○ **PLAN**
Choose a gadget to review. Complete the word web.

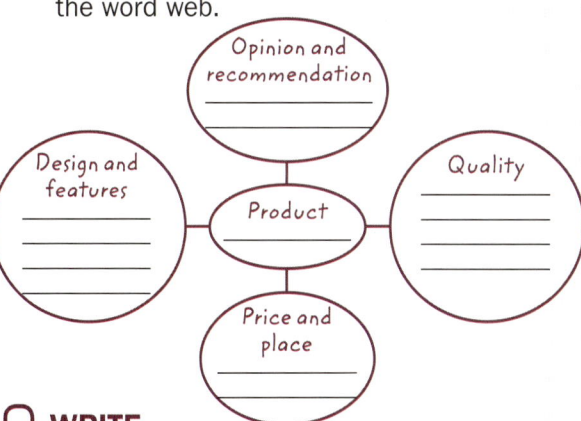

○ **WRITE**
Write your product review. Use your notes to help you. Include the parts of a product review and *while* and *whereas* to make comparisons. Write at least 150 words.

○ **CHECK**
Check your writing. Can you answer "yes" to these questions?

- Is information from the Focus on Content box in your review?
- Do you use *while* and *whereas* correctly to make comparisons?

Workbook, pp. 40–41

Before There Was Texting

Our world today is filled with gadgets that make our lives easier – and paperless! The invention of the Internet has also decreased our use of paper. We send emails and text messages electronically, and we sometimes do our homework online. We don't even think about the importance of paper. Whereas the Internet has helped us communicate in today's world, paper has been helping people communicate for centuries.

Writing existed before paper, but it was difficult. People wrote on clay tablets, shells, bones, and pieces of wood. Then paper came along and changed the world – slowly. The exact date of the invention of paper isn't known, but people in Egypt made paper about 5,000 years ago. Very thin pieces of papyrus plants were cut to be used as paper. Even though the word *paper* comes from *papyrus*, this invention didn't travel far. It wasn't until about 2,000 years ago that paper started to travel the globe. Historians say that Cai Lun, a Chinese court official, was tired of carrying his books. During his time, books were written on pieces of bamboo, and they were extremely heavy. Cai Lun found a way to make paper from small pieces of bark from trees. He mixed them with water and pounded them with a wooden tool. Finally, he put them on cloth to let the water dry. The end result – a thin sheet of paper! After Cai Lun's invention, papermaking quickly spread throughout Asia, to places like Korea and Japan. About 1,000 years later, papermaking made its way to India, and in the 11th century, to Europe. In the late 1600s, people in what is now the United States were making paper. It wasn't until the 1800s, when paper factories started in Australia, that paper had made it all the way around the world.

Paper was one of the first tools used to help people spread information – through books, letters, and newspapers. You could say that paper was the world's first communication gadget!

Culture: An article about the invention of paper

1. Look at the title. Why do you think paper is an important invention?

2. Read and listen to the article. Number the photos in the article in the correct order.

3. Read the article again. Correct the sentences.
   1. The Internet ~~increased~~ *decreased* the amount of paper we use.
   2. Before paper, people wrote on clay tablets, shells, bones, and pieces of plants.
   3. People made paper in Egypt about 2,000 years ago.
   4. Cai Lun invented paper because he didn't like writing in books.
   5. Cai Lun mixed pieces of tree bark and cloth to make paper.
   6. Paper could be found all over the world in the 1600s.

4. **YOUR TURN** Work with a partner. What other inventions changed the world? How did they change things?

DID YOU KNOW…?

People wrote on silk cloth in China before paper was invented, but it was far too expensive for most people.

BE CURIOUS Find out about the history of the Internet. In what ways did the Internet change over time? (Workbook, p. 83)

6.3 THE START OF THE WEB

UNIT 6 REVIEW

Vocabulary

1. Read the sentences. Write the missing words in the puzzle. Find out what Lorenzo needs to get by filling in the gray boxes.

   1. S W I T C H
   2.
   3.
   4.
   5.
   6.
   7.

   1. Can you find the ___ to turn off this lamp?
   2. Those energy-efficient ___ bulbs are kind of expensive.
   3. The blades in that old ___ look dangerous.
   4. Can you turn on the ___? It's so cold in here.
   5. The ___ to my computer doesn't fit in the wall socket.
   6. Do you have any ___ so that I can light this candle?
   7. I'm so excited about my new ___ conditioner because it has a remote control.

Grammar

2. Put the words in the correct order to make sentences.

   1. to / Chao / expected / for his work / paid / be
      _____
   2. by our friends / liked / be / to / we / want
      _____
   3. be / the invention / needs / by January / finished / to
      _____
   4. locked / the doors / be / at 9:00 p.m. / are / to
      _____

3. Write sentences with *get/have* something done. Use the tense in the parentheses for the main verb.

   1. I / have / my teeth / clean / next week (present continuous)
      _____
   2. Elsa / not have / her house / paint / this year (future with *will*)
      _____
   3. they / get / their skateboards / fix / before the competition (past perfect)
      _____

Useful language

4. Complete the conversation.

   | Could you show me | Does it have | Is it … to use? |
   | How long does | How good is | Which model is |

   Anne: ¹_____ some air conditioners, please?
   Clerk: Sure. What would you like to see?
   Anne: ²_____ the cheapest?
   Clerk: The Saver500 is the cheapest.
   Anne: ³_____ difficult _____
   Clerk: Oh, no. Not at all.
   Anne: ⁴_____ a remote control?
   Clerk: No, I'm sorry. It doesn't.
   Anne: Oh, OK. ⁵_____ the cooling system?
   Clerk: It's very good. And the Saver500 is on sale!
   Anne: Really? ⁶_____ the sale last?
   Clerk: Until Saturday.

PROGRESS CHECK: Now I can . . .

- ☐ talk about everyday objects and why they're important.
- ☐ talk about new uses for everyday objects.
- ☐ talk about inventions.
- ☐ ask and answer questions about buying a gadget.
- ☐ write a product review for a gadget.
- ☐ talk about how inventions have changed the world.

CLIL PROJECT

6.4 INSIDE THE GUITAR, p. 118

UNITS 5–6 REVIEW, Workbook, pp. 42–43

7 Have a Ball!

Discovery EDUCATION

BE CURIOUS

Let's Celebrate

What's the worst party you've ever been to?

Like Father, Like Daughter

1. What is this woman doing?

2. Why do you think she's doing this?

3. Do you have a similar celebration in your country? What is it for?

UNIT CONTENTS

Vocabulary Celebration phrases; Descriptive adjectives
Grammar Verb + -ing form (gerund) or infinitive; -ing form (gerund) as subject; by/for + -ing form
Listening Surprising celebrations

Vocabulary: Celebration phrases

1. Match the phrases with the correct pictures.

a. dress up
b. give a present
✓ c. have a good time
d. hold a contest
e. play music
f. prepare special food
g. put up decorations
h. set off fireworks
i. watch a parade

1. _c_
2. ___
3. ___
4. ___
5. ___
6. ___
7. ___
8. ___
9. ___

2. Listen, check, and repeat.

3. Complete the paragraph with the phrases from Exercise 1.

This year, I'm going to have a New Year's Eve party. I'm going to ¹ _put up decorations_ in my home. They'll be black, white, and silver. I'm also going to ² _____, like some great desserts that my parents will help me make. I'm going to ask all of my friends to ³ _____ for the party. You know, wear fancy dresses and suits. I'll also ⁴ _____ – the best-dressed person gets a prize! Of course, I'll ⁵ _____ at the party. I've already downloaded my favorite songs of this year. At night, my older brother will ⁶ _____ – just small ones, of course. They'll look great in the night sky. I'm sure everyone is going to ⁷ _____. It will be the best party ever! My best friend is going to stay the night. It's her birthday the next day, so I'll ⁸ _____ her _____. I bought her a new case for her phone. Then we're going to ⁹ _____ downtown. The city has one every year on New Year's Day.

Speaking: How do you have a good time?

4. YOUR TURN Work with a partner. When do you do the things in Exercise 1? Tell your partner. Ask each other follow-up questions.

My school holds a talent contest every year.

Have you ever entered it?

Yes, I have. Last year, my friends and I dressed up as rock stars and sang a song.

Did you have a good time?

Workbook, p. 44

Reading How to Plan a Party; A Great Family Party!; Korea: Coming of Age
Conversation Making exclamations
Writing A description of a celebration

PARTY Planning

HOW TO PLAN A PARTY

Everybody loves going to parties! But some people don't enjoy hosting them because it can be very stressful. Are you planning to have a party? Read these how-to tips to make party planning easy!

1. **Choose the time, date, and place.** Give your guests advanced notice. Teens have busy lives, and you want to make sure the most people possible can come. Decide how many people you are going to invite before you pick the place. Will they all fit at your house? Do you need to have the party at a bigger place, like a park or a restaurant?

2. **Pick a theme.** Is it a party for a birthday, holiday, or other special occasion? Are you having a "just because" party? Consider having a theme party. For example, ask guests to dress up as their favorite cartoon characters or super heroes. Maybe the theme is related to the time of year, like "Winter Wonderland," "Think Spring," or "Summer Blast."

3. **Plan your party.** Decide what food you want to make and if you are going to put up decorations. Are you going to hold a contest or have games? Will you play music at the party or have a band? If you have a theme party, you can plan your party around the theme. For example, for a "Winter Wonderland" party, you might put up decorations of snowflakes and snowmen. You might serve cold foods, like ice cream. Don't forget to plan a budget. Figure out how much everything is going to cost. Are you going to buy food, make food, or ask your friends to bring something to share?

4. **Invite your friends.** Send out invitations. You can send emails, texts, or make an invitation to post online. Be sure to let your friends know whether or not they can invite guests. You don't want to invite 20 people and have 40 show up!

With a little planning, your party is sure to be successful, and you'll enjoy the party as much as your friends do!

Reading: A how-to article about planning a party

1. Look at the pictures and the title. What do you think you will learn from this article?

2. Read and listen to the article. Number the steps in order.
   ____ Plan the menu and activities for your party.
   ____ Decide what kind of party you are going to have.
   ____ Tell your friends about the party.
   ____ Decide when and where you are going to have the party.

3. Read the article again. Then read the sentences. Which steps from Exercise 2 are the people following? Write 1, 2, 3, or 4.
   1. Carrie is going to have her guests play card games. ____
   2. Leo decided to have his party at a skate park. ____
   3. Tom is having his guests dress up in sports uniforms. ____
   4. Luke is having his party on April 16. ____
   5. Jing posted an invitation on her Web page. ____
   6. Sylvia is going to have her brother's band play music at the party. ____
   7. Patricia is having a "Back to School" party. ____

4. **YOUR TURN** Work with a partner. Have you ever planned a party? What was it like? What kinds of parties do you like to go to?

DID YOU KNOW...?
Some people pay party planners to plan parties for them. Party planners are popular for big events like weddings, special birthday parties, and graduations.

Grammar: Verb + -ing form (gerund) or infinitive

5. Complete the chart.

Many verbs are followed by the -ing form of a verb or an infinitive. Some verbs can be followed by either an -ing form or an infinitive with no change in meaning. Others can be followed by either an -ing form or an infinitive, but the meaning changes.

Verb + -ing form:	**Consider having** a theme party.
consider discuss enjoy finish keep miss	Some people **don't enjoy** _____ them.
Verb + infinitive:	Decide what food you **want** _____. Do you **need to have** the party at a bigger place?
decide learn expect need plan want	
Verb + -ing form or infinitive:	Everybody **loves** _____ to parties! Everybody **loves to go** to parties!
begin hate like love prefer start	
Verb + -ing form or infinitive with change in meaning:	Don't **forget** _____ a budget. (= not forget to do something) I'll never **forget going** to my first birthday party. (= not forgetting that something happened)
forget remember try	

> Check your answers: Grammar reference, p. 112

6. Circle the correct answers. Sometimes both answers are possible.
1. I like **going** / **to go** to parties on the weekends.
2. Remember **inviting** / **to invite** Susan to your party.
3. I prefer **watching** / **to watch** parades on TV.
4. We plan **dressing up** / **to dress up** for the holiday party.
5. The city decided **setting off** / **to set off** fireworks on Friday night.
6. Sarah finished **putting up** / **to put up** decorations at 9:00 p.m.

7. Write sentences. Use the simple past and -ing forms (gerunds) or infinitives.
1. I / learn / play / the violin six years ago
   I learned to play the violin six years ago.
2. we / discuss / prepare / special food for the party
   _____
3. Terry / start / take / photos at the graduation ceremony
   _____
4. Emily / expect / hear / from her cousin last week
   _____
5. They / hate / go / home after a school party
   _____

 *Say it* **RIGHT!**

When a verb is followed by an infinitive, **to** usually sounds like *ta* and isn't stressed. Listen to the sentences.
*I learned **to** play the violin six years ago. My parents love **to** hear me play.*
Work with a partner. Read the sentences in Exercise 7. Practice reducing **to**.

Speaking: An end-of-school party

8. YOUR TURN Work in groups. Design your ideal school-leaving party. What type of party will it be? Formal or informal? Make a list of the activities.

> I can't imagine having a formal party. Let's make it informal.

> But dressing up would be fun!

9. YOUR TURN Present your party to the class. Which party sounds the most fun?

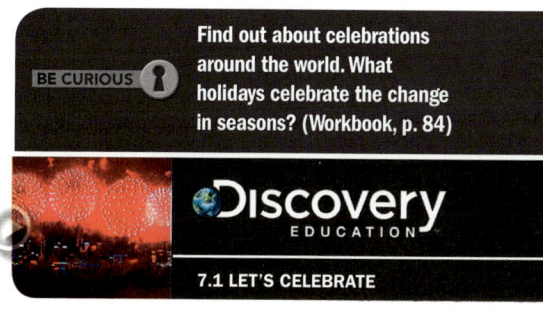

Find out about celebrations around the world. What holidays celebrate the change in seasons? (Workbook, p. 84)

7.1 LET'S CELEBRATE

Let's CELEBRATE!

Listening: Surprising celebrations

1. Have you ever been to an unusual celebration or festival? What was it for? What was it like?

2. Listen to a show about some unusual celebrations. Circle the correct answers.
   1. The festival in Harbin, China, has **artwork** / **fireworks**.
   2. For the festival in Ivrea, Italy, people throw about **4,000** / **1,000,000** oranges.
   3. The festival in Lopburi, Thailand, starts **in the morning** / **at night**.

3. Listen again. Match the places (1–3) with the correct sentences (a–f).
   1. Harbin ____ ____   2. Ivrea ____ ____   3. Lopburi ____ ____

   a. There's singing and dancing.
   b. It's amazing at night.
   c. People feed animals.
   d. People dress up in costumes.
   e. The weather is cold.
   f. It celebrates a past event.

Vocabulary: Descriptive adjectives

4. Replace the underlined words with the correct words. Then listen and check.

colorful	lively	peaceful	traditional
crowded	messy	scary	
✓ impressive	noisy	stunning	

   1. The dancers at the festival were ~~amazing and extremely talented~~ *impressive*.
   2. Jana's dress is <u>blue, yellow, green, red, and pink</u>.
   3. The street was so <u>full of people</u> that I couldn't find a good place to watch the parade.
   4. We made the party <u>exciting and full of energy</u> by playing music.
   5. Our house was <u>dirty</u> after the party, and we spent the next day cleaning it up.
   6. The fireworks were very <u>loud</u>. My little sister hated them.
   7. Last year, there was a fight at our New Year's party, but this year it was <u>calm and quiet</u>.
   8. My friend had a costume party, and I wore something <u>that made people afraid</u> – I dressed up as a vampire.
   9. The sand sculptures for the contest were <u>very beautiful</u>. They were so beautiful that they made me speechless.
   10. We learned some <u>old and historic</u> dances for a school play about our country.

5. **YOUR TURN** Work with a partner. Which celebration would you like to go to the most? Why?

   > I'd like to go to the festival in Lopburi because it seems lively and . . .

68 | Unit 7

Grammar: -ing form (gerund) as subject; by/for + -ing form

6. Complete the chart.

> You can use the -ing form as the subject of a sentence. When it's the subject, the verb is singular.
>
> **Traveling** to Italy is always great.
> **Watch**_____ the monkeys is very entertaining.
> **Not going** to the festival would be a mistake.
>
> The -ing form can also be used after *by* to show how to do something and after *for* to show the purpose or use of something.
>
> Let's start _____ **returning** to Harbin.
> The weather is perfect **for making** ice statues.

> Check your answers: Grammar reference, p. 112

The Sundance Film Festival takes place in Sundance, Colorado, every year. The movies shown at the festival do not have big budgets like Hollywood movies.

7. Write sentences using gerunds as subjects.

1. go / to the Sundance Film Festival / be / my favorite thing to do
   Going to the Sundance Film Festival is my favorite thing to do.

2. show / independent films at Sundance / support / talented directors, writers, and actors
   _____

3. have / a movie / at Sundance / be / a great honor
   _____

4. not arrive late / to a Sundance movie / help / you get a better seat
   _____

5. watch / Sundance movies / make / me happy
   _____

8. Complete the sentences with the -ing form of the verbs and by or for.

1. The city used an open field ___*for setting off*___ (set off) fireworks.
2. I mostly use my new smartphone _____ (take) photos.
3. We'll start the party _____ (play) music.
4. We'll celebrate the New Year _____ (watch) a parade.
5. Let's make the room look special _____ (put up) decorations.
6. The community park is a great place _____ (have) a family reunion.

Speaking: A lively celebration

9. YOUR TURN Work with a partner. Ask and answer questions about a festival, celebration, or other event you've been to.

1. What was the event? What was it like?
2. What was your reason for going?
3. How did going to the event make you feel?
4. What would others experience and learn by going to the event?

> *I went to the Garlic Festival in the park last summer. Going to the event made me want to eat garlic! It was crowded and . . .*

> Workbook, pp. 46–47

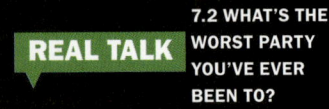 **REAL TALK** 7.2 WHAT'S THE WORST PARTY YOU'VE EVER BEEN TO?

Party *Time!*

Conversation: Planning a party is difficult.

1. **REAL TALK** Watch or listen to the teenagers talk about the worst parties they've been to. Match the parties (1–6) with the reasons the parties were bad (a–f).

   1. ____ A party last month
   2. ____ A spring dance
   3. ____ Someone's own party
   4. ____ A wedding reception
   5. ____ A costume party
   6. ____ A best friend's birthday

   a. Parents staying for the movie
   b. A chocolate fountain not working correctly
   c. Getting the day wrong
   d. Dressing up for the wrong theme
   e. Not being able to play music
   f. Having to cancel the party

2. **YOUR TURN** What's the worst party *you've* ever been to? Tell your partner.

3. Listen to Drew helping Ellen plan her birthday party. Complete the conversation.

USEFUL LANGUAGE: Exclamations

| Great idea! | How | ✓ is so | That'd be | That's such a | What a |

Ellen: It's my birthday next week, and I haven't done anything for the party yet. I don't want it to be the worst party ever. Planning a party ¹ _is so_ difficult!

Drew: Don't worry. I'll help you. What needs to be done?

Ellen: Well, I haven't decided what music to play.

Drew: I have tons of music. I can organize a playlist at home and bring it.

Ellen: ² _____ great! Thanks.

Drew: What about food? Do you know what you're going to have?

Ellen: Well, I decided to have a rainbow theme. Maybe the food could have something to do with that.

Drew: ³ _____ cool theme! You could have food the color of the rainbow. Red cake, yellow and orange vegetables, things like that.

Ellen: ⁴ _____ good idea! Let's make a list. And we can make a list of decorations, too.

Drew: ⁵ _____ I'll help you put up the decorations the day before the party.

Ellen: ⁶ _____ nice of you! Thanks.

Drew: No problem. I love planning parties.

Ellen: I'm feeling better about it, thanks to you. Let's start working on those lists.

4. Practice the conversation with a partner.

5. **YOUR TURN** Work with a partner. Take turns helping each other plan a party or event. Use one of the items below or your own ideas.

   | a class trip | a holiday party |
   | a pool party | a school dance |

70 | Unit 7

💬 A Great Family Party!

posted by Amy Jackson | January 15

My grandparents were born on the same day. Last July, they were 70 years old, so we had a party with family, friends, and neighbors. The party was in my grandparents' yard because their house is too small for a big party. We did everything ourselves. My mom and dad prepared special food, and my cousins and I put up decorations.

First we had lunch at the party, and the food was so delicious! After eating, we watched a film my aunt had made with photos and videos of my grandparents. Then my little brother played "Happy Birthday" on his guitar. He was so nervous, but my grandparents loved listening to it. He played it again, and everyone sang. Finally, everyone gave my grandparents presents.

At night, we danced to my grandparents' favorite music. The party was so amazing! I wanted to dance all night, but I was too tired.

Reading to write: A description of a celebration

6. Look at the title and the photo. What do you think Amy and her family celebrated? Read her description to check.

   ### ⊙ Focus on CONTENT
   When you write a description of a celebration, include this information:
   - the reason for the celebration
   - the place of the celebration
   - how you prepared for it
   - what happened at the celebration

7. Read Amy's description again. What information does she include for each category in the Focus on Content box?

   ### ⊙ Focus on LANGUAGE
   Use *so* + adjective to emphasize an adjective.
   *The party was **so lively**!*

   Use *too* + adjective to say there was more than needed or wanted.
   *We didn't set off fireworks at the party because it was **too dangerous**.*

8. Find the sentences in Amy's description with *so* and *too*.

9. Complete the sentences with *too* when possible. When it's not possible, use *so*.

   | crowded | delicious | exciting | noisy | scary | slow |

   1. The dance was _____! We had a great time dancing and talking with friends.
   2. The festival was _____. You couldn't walk down the streets.
   3. We couldn't dance because the music was _____.
   4. My aunt and uncle prepared special food for the party. It tasted _____.
   5. We couldn't talk to each other because the party was _____.
   6. I screamed when I saw Connor. His costume was _____!

Writing: Your celebration

○ **PLAN**
Choose a celebration to describe and take notes.

Celebration	
The reason	
The place	
How you prepared for it	
What happened	

○ **WRITE**
Write a description of a celebration. Use your notes to help you. Use *so* and *too*. Write at least 150 words.

○ **CHECK**
Check your writing. Can you answer "yes" to these questions?
- Is information from the Focus on Content box in your description?
- Do you use *so* and *too* correctly?

➤ Get it RIGHT!
Be careful not to confuse *so* and *too*. Sometimes a sentence works with both words, but they have different meanings.
*She is **so** happy.* = She is very happy.
*She is **too** happy.* = She should be sadder.

Workbook, pp. 48–49

Korea: COMING OF AGE

Many cultures celebrate "coming of age." This expression means that you go from being a child to becoming an adult. In Latino cultures, this happens for girls at 15 with *quinceañera* parties. Many teens in the United States have "sweet sixteen" parties. In Jewish cultures, boys and girls have *bar mitzvahs* and *bat mitzvahs* when they turn 13. In Korea, on the third Monday of May, 19-year-olds celebrate their Coming of Age Day in the year they turn 20.

In some ways, it is a very serious and symbolic day. The soon-to-be ex-teenagers are acknowledged as adult members of society. They are reminded of the responsibility and pride involved in leading the future of Korea. Coming of age also means teens can do things that adults do, like voting, driving, and getting married.

Participants wear traditional Korean clothing, known as *hanbok*. The clothes are bright and colorful. Men often tie their hair into knots on top of their heads and wear traditional hats made of bamboo and horsehair, called *gat*. Women roll their braided hair into a bun, which is held in place with a *binyeo*, a long, decorative hairpin.

During the ceremony, the young people often sit in the center of a stadium, boys on one side and girls on the other. The children bow to their parents out of respect. In turn, the parents also bow to their children to recognize their children's promise to be responsible adult citizens. And then there's the fun part – people give the "new adults" presents. For girls, the most popular presents are jewelry, bags, flowers, and makeup. Boys often get watches or electric shavers.

The ceremony is hundreds of years old, and it was popular between the 1300s and 1900s. The ceremony became popular again in the 1970s. Parents fear that the traditional coming-of-age day festival is being lost in Korea. Many young Koreans think 20 is too old to become an adult. They feel like they are adults already and don't take part in the ceremony. Other young people decide to have more modern versions of the ceremony. For those who do participate, it is an extremely important and exciting day.

Culture: An article about coming of age in Korea

1. Look at the photos. How old do you think the people are? What are they wearing?

2. Read and listen to the article. What is the Korean celebration? Why is it important?

3. Read the article again. Circle the correct answers.
   1. People around the world celebrate becoming an adult at **the same / (different)** ages.
   2. In Korea, people are considered adults at age **19 / 20**.
   3. The boys and girls wear **traditional / modern** hairstyles.
   4. The children bow to their parents out of **responsibility / respect**.
   5. The ceremony was started again in the **1300s / 1970s**.

4. **YOUR TURN** Work with a partner. Discuss the questions.
   1. At what age are people in your country considered adults? Are there any coming-of-age celebrations or traditions?
   2. At what age can you do these things in your country: vote, drive, get married?

DID YOU KNOW…?
In some cultures in Australia, boys are sent on a "walkabout" as a coming-of-age tradition. They must survive outdoors for 6 months.

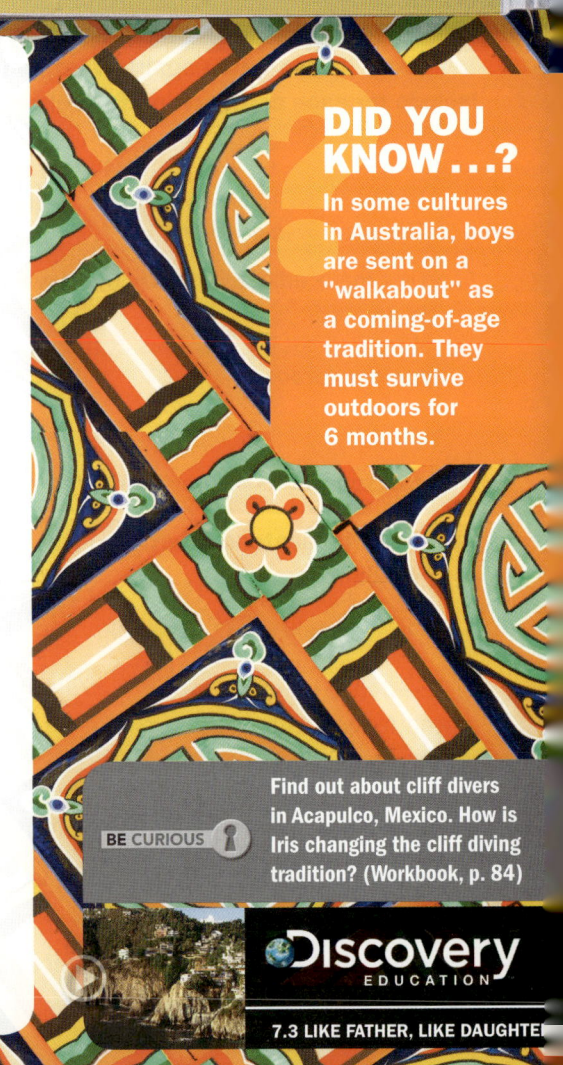

BE CURIOUS Find out about cliff divers in Acapulco, Mexico. How is Iris changing the cliff diving tradition? (Workbook, p. 84)

Discovery EDUCATION

7.3 LIKE FATHER, LIKE DAUGHTER

UNIT 7 REVIEW

Vocabulary

1. What are the objects used for? Label the pictures with the correct phrases.

dress up	give a present
play music	prepare special food
put up decorations	set off fireworks

1. _____

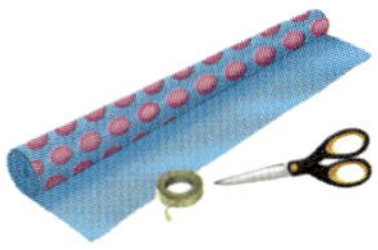

2. _____

3. _____

4. _____

5. _____

6. _____

Grammar

2. Complete the sentences with -ing forms (gerunds) or infinitives.

1. Will you consider _____ (come) to my party?
2. Gina forgot _____ (lock) the door.
3. We thought the festival would be peaceful, but it began _____ (get) so noisy.
4. I miss _____ (go) to school dances now that I've graduated.

3. Correct the mistakes.

1. Seeing the Battle of the Oranges were impressive.
2. We raised money for our school for holding a talent contest.
3. No spending money on decorations was a great way to save money.
4. We got around the crowded festival for walking on side streets.
5. Give presents is my favorite part of celebrating the holiday season.
6. My sister gets paid by singing at birthday parties.

Useful language

4. Circle the correct exclamations.

1. **A:** Let's go watch the parade tomorrow.
   B: _____ idea!
   a. Great b. How

2. **A:** Are you done planning your party?
   B: No. Budgeting _____!
   a. that'd be difficult b. is so difficult

3. **A:** Look at my costume for the festival.
   B: _____ a colorful dress!
   a. What b. It's so

4. **A:** Let's have a party for Father's Day.
   B: _____ nice.
   a. What b. That'd be

5. **A:** I want to set off fireworks tonight.
   B: _____ bad idea! It's so dangerous.
   a. That's such a b. Great

6. **A:** I just won a dance contest.
   B: _____ impressive!
   a. How b. What an

PROGRESS CHECK: Now I can . . .

☐ talk about party preparations and activities.
☐ plan an end-of-school party.
☐ describe events and festivals.
☐ comment using exclamations.
☐ write a description of a celebration.
☐ talk about coming-of-age celebrations.

8 Mysteries and Secrets

A Lost Civilization

What's the biggest lie you've ever been told?

Mysteries of the Brain

Reliving History

1. What is the scuba diver doing?

2. What do you think the diver will learn?

3. What mysteries do you know about?

UNIT CONTENTS
Vocabulary Adjectives with *un-*; Reporting verbs
Grammar Time clauses; Present participle clauses; Reported speech; Indirect questions
Listening A mysterious act of kindness

Vocabulary: Adjectives with un-

1. **Complete the sentences. Add un- to the words.**

✓ believable	known	necessary
expected	likely	solved
important	lucky	usual

   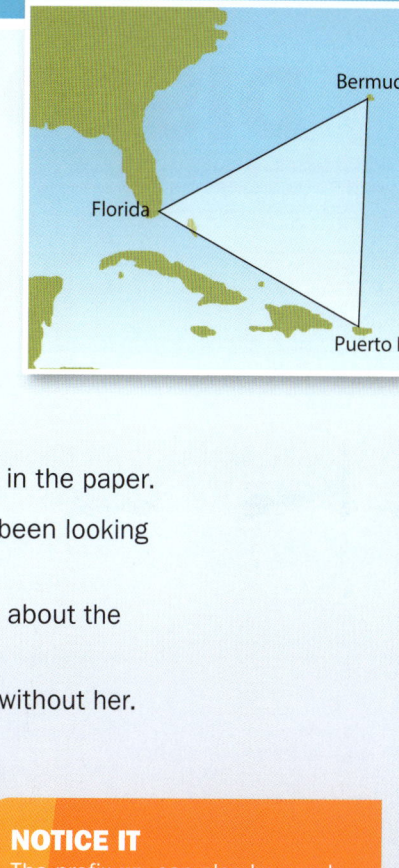

   1. The stories about the Bermuda Triangle are <u>unbelievable</u>! I can't imagine that so many ships were lost in that part of the ocean.
   2. The hurricane was _____. We had no idea it was coming.
   3. The news about the storm was so _____ that it wasn't even in the paper.
   4. The location of the sailboat is _____. Rescue workers have been looking for it for 2 days.
   5. It's _____ that we will ever know everything there is to know about the ocean, but researchers are constantly uncovering its secrets.
   6. The scuba diver was sick the day her dive team saw a giant squid without her. She was _____.
   7. Bringing our swimsuits to the beach was _____. We weren't able to swim because there were sharks in the water.
   8. The Loch Ness monster is one of the world's _____ mysteries. No one has proven that it exists.
   9. Dan saw an _____ animal in the water. It was very strange, and he had never seen anything like it before.

   > **NOTICE IT**
   > The prefix *un-* can also be used before verbs to give an opposite meaning.
   > **un**cover   **un**do   **un**lock   **un**pack

 2. **Listen, check, and repeat.**

Speaking: Unusual events

3. **YOUR TURN** Work with a partner. Use the adjectives in Exercise 1 with and without *un-* to describe one of the following situations. Ask each other questions.

Situations	Questions
a dream you had recently	What happened (next)?
a mystery you heard or read about	What was it like?
recent extreme weather	How did you/he/she/it feel?
an interesting book or movie you've seen	When did you have/see/read/hear about it?

   > I had an unusual dream last night.

   > What happened?

   > I was in charge of an important event. I had to unlock the door to a room, but the key was too small.

   > What happened next?

   > This part is unbelievable! The . . .

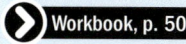 Workbook, p. 50

Reading A Secret Under the Street; The Secret Room; An Unbelievable Book
Conversation Confirming and denying
Writing A story about a secret

DISCOVERIES

A SECRET UNDER THE STREET

The Atlantic Avenue Tunnel was made in 1844 before the subway system was created in New York City. Steam trains traveling between New York City and Boston went through the tunnel. The trains drove by Atlantic Avenue in Brooklyn, New York, coming in and out of the tunnel. As Brooklyn got busier, the train became more dangerous to people walking on the street. So, in 1861, steam trains were no longer allowed in the city, and the tunnel was closed.

It's 1980. Bob Diamond, a 19-year-old engineering student, is on a mission to uncover a secret. He hears a story on a radio program about the unused tunnel that is under the very busy street in Brooklyn, where he lives. Bob is excited when he hears that John Wilkes Booth, the man who killed President Lincoln in 1865, might have hidden pages from his journal in the abandoned tunnel. After hearing about the mysterious tunnel, he decides to start looking for it.

Bob finds an old map with the tunnel on it after searching city records for 8 months. It shows a circle above the tunnel, and Bob thinks it might be an entrance. When Bob goes to the place on the map, he finds a manhole cover and convinces men from a gas company to let him go down the hole. He crawls underground until he hits a brick wall. He knocks down part of the wall, and he's hit with unexpected cold air. It's the tunnel!

Bob's discovery is unbelievable! He never finds John Wilkes Booth's journal, but the tunnel is exciting enough. After the news spreads, he becomes a local hero. The city puts him in charge of the tunnel. He starts giving tours and also starts the Brooklyn Historic Railway Association. As soon as he found the tunnel, he knew he had to share it with others, and he wants to make this unknown city secret known to all!

Reading: An article about an old train tunnel

1. Look at the pictures. What do you think the man discovered? How old do you think it is?

2. Read and listen to the article. What is the purpose of the article?

   a. to inform the reader about secret train tunnels in cities

   b. to tell a story about a man's search for and discovery of a secret tunnel

   c. to give information about transportation in New York City in the past

3. Read the article again. Are the sentences true or false? Write *T* (true), *F* (false), or *NI* (no information).

   1. Bob Diamond wanted to become a train engineer. _____
   2. Bob does a lot of research to find the train tunnel. _____
   3. A subway replaced the Atlantic Avenue Tunnel. _____
   4. It took Bob more than a year to find the tunnel. _____
   5. Bob found a secret journal of a famous person in the tunnel. _____
   6. Bob gave tours of the tunnel to inform people about its history. _____

4. **YOUR TURN** Work with a partner. What things can you visit to learn about the past in your area? Were any of the things discovered in recent times?

> **DID YOU KNOW...?**
> Bob Diamond and others believe there is an old steam train buried in another part of the tunnel.

Grammar: Time clauses; present participle clauses

5. Complete the chart.

Use time clauses to show the order of events in the past, present, and future.
Use **before** to show that the event in the time clause happened second.
The Atlantic Avenue Tunnel was made in 1844, _____ the subway system was created.
FIRST EVENT — SECOND EVENT
Use **after** to show the event in the time clause happened first.
_____ the news spreads, Bob becomes a local hero.
FIRST EVENT — SECOND EVENT
Use **when** to show that both events happened at the same time.
They will search for a steam train in the tunnel _____ they have enough money.
You can use the **-ing** form (gerund) of a verb after **before** and **after**.
Before searching for the tunnel, Bob heard about it on a radio program. Bob finds an old map **after** _____ city records for 8 months.

> **Get it RIGHT!**
> When talking about the future, the time clause is usually in the present tense, not the future with **will**.
> **When** they **have** enough money, they'll search for the steam train. (NOT: **When** they **will have** enough money, they'll search for the steam train.)

▶ Check your answers: Grammar reference, p. 113

6. Put the words in the correct order to make sentences.

1. an hour before / had waited / we / for / the tunnel / we saw *We had waited for an hour before we saw the tunnel.*
2. we / visit / seeing the tunnel, / the museum / after / will _____
3. the ancient pyramids / go to Mexico / we / will / when we / visit _____
4. online after / Maria usually / secret caves / posts photos / exploring _____

7. Circle the correct answers.

Scientists thought there were nine planets in our solar system ¹(**until**) / **every time** they discovered a tenth planet with a telescope. Scientists called the unnamed planet *2003 UB313* ²**while / before** they gave it its official name – Eris. ³**After / Before** they found Eris in 2003, they took photos of it. ⁴**When / Until** they studied the photos, they thought Eris was bigger than Pluto. However, they realized this wasn't true ⁵**every time / once** they did more research. Scientists have been discussing what the definition of a planet is ⁶**since / as** 2003, when Eris was discovered. Eris is now considered a dwarf planet. ⁷**As soon as / Until** news about Eris was shared with the world, people wanted to know about the tenth planet.

> **Other times clauses can be used to show:**
> - events happening at the same time: **while**, **as**
> - one event quickly following another: **as soon as**, **once**
> - when an action started in the past: **since**
> - an action continuing up to another action: **until**
> - repeated events are connected: **every time**

Speaking: My discovery

8. YOUR TURN Work with a partner. Pretend you made a discovery. Use one of the ideas below or your own idea. Tell your partner how you found it and what you'll do with it.

| an old book | a secret cave | a new star |

> *I found an old book while I was cleaning our basement. Once I figure out how much it's worth, I will . . .*

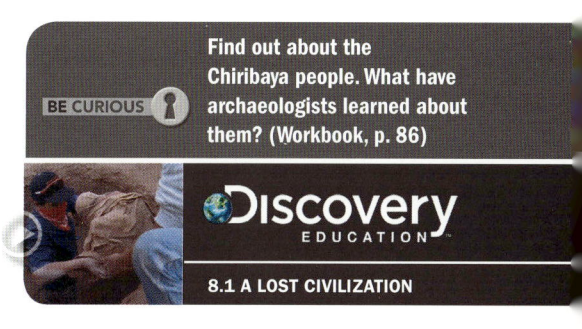

Find out about the Chiribaya people. What have archaeologists learned about them? (Workbook, p. 86)

BE CURIOUS

Discovery EDUCATION
8.1 A LOST CIVILIZATION

Workbook, pp. 50–51

Unit 8 | 77

Solving MYSTERIES

Listening: A mysterious act of kindness

1. Have you heard about any mysterious things happening in your neighborhood or town? What were they?

2. Listen to Jill and Vic talking about a mysterious neighborhood event. What's the mystery?

3. Listen again. Circle the correct answers.
   1. Dolls were given to **two / eight** girls in the neighborhood.
   2. Vic's sister **kept / didn't keep** her doll.
   3. The person leaving the dolls **was / wasn't** leaving notes.
   4. **Vic / Jill** found out who was leaving the dolls.
   5. There was a clue **online / by the front of a door**.
   6. Vic **is / isn't** going to tell others the secret.

Vocabulary: Reporting verbs

4. Match the verbs (1–9) with the definitions (a–i). Then listen and check.

   1. admit ___f___
   2. agree _____
   3. claim _____
   4. decide _____
   5. insist _____
   6. mention _____
   7. recommend _____
   8. reply _____
   9. write _____

   a. to say something briefly
   b. to put words on paper or on a computer
   c. to suggest something to someone
   d. to have the same opinion as someone else
   e. to answer someone
   f. to say that you did something
   g. to choose something after thinking about the possibilities
   h. to say something firmly, especially when others don't agree
   i. to state that something is true without proof

5. **YOUR TURN** Work with a partner. Think of things you and people you know said or wrote recently and tell your partner. Use the reporting verbs in Exercise 4.

   > My sister insisted that I took her laptop. So, I finally admitted that I had taken it.

78 | Unit 8

Grammar: Reported speech; indirect questions

6. Complete the chart.

Use reported speech and reported questions to tell others what another person said. In both reported speech and reported questions, the verbs usually change tenses.

Quoted speech	Reported speech
She said, "I **am leaving** the dolls."	She admitted that she **was leaving** the dolls.
She said, "I **was watching** TV."	She wrote that she _____ **been watching** TV.
He asked, "**When will** you **be talking** to her?"	He asked me **when I would be** _____ to her.
He asked, "**Are** you **keeping** her secret?"	He asked me **if I was keeping** her secret.

Infinitives can be used with these reporting verbs: agree, claim, decide.

| I **agreed to keep** it a secret. | She **claimed** _____ **know** who had done it. |

The **-ing** form can be used with these reporting verbs: recommend, insist on, admit to.

| She **insisted** _____ **keeping** the doll. | I **recommend posting** a question online. |

Imperative clauses

Change an imperative to a reported imperative using infinitive verbs.

Quoted imperative	Reported imperative
He said, "**Tell** me about it!"	He told her **to tell** him about it.
She said, "**Don't tell** anyone."	She said **not** _____ anyone.

> Check your answers: Grammar reference, p. 113

7. Change the direct speech to reported speech.

1. "I'll be going to a detective school." (she / mention)
   She mentioned that she would be going to a detective school.

2. "I was reading a mystery book all day."
   (she / claim)
   _____

3. "We'll solve this mystery." (they / insist on + -ing form)
   _____

4. "Don't look in that closet." (he / say)
   _____

5. "Are you trying to solve the mystery?"
   (he / ask us)
   _____

6. "Tell me the ending of the story." (I / say)
   _____

8. Write indirect questions for the witness of a robbery.

1. What's your name?
   Can you tell me your name?

2. What happened?
   _____

3. When did the robbery take place?
   _____

4. Did you do anything to try to stop the robbers?
   _____

5. Were you frightened?
   _____

Indirect Questions

Can you tell me . . . ?, *Could you tell me . . . ?*, *I wonder . . .* , and *I don't know* are used to form indirect questions.

Direct	Indirect
What's going on?	**Can you tell me** what's going on?
Why was she doing it?	**I wonder** why she was doing it.
Did she admit to the crime?	**I don't know** if she admitted to the crime.

  Say it **RIGHT!**

Listen to the indirect questions. Notice the rising and falling intonation.
Can you tell me what happened?
I wonder what happened.
Pay attention to the way you pronounce indirect questions in Exercise 9.

Speaking: Where were you last night?

9. YOUR TURN Make notes about an imaginary crime you saw. Work with a partner. Student A is a police officer and Student B is a witness. Use the questions in Exercise 8 and your own ideas to ask and answer questions about what you saw. Then swap roles.

> Workbook, pp. 52–53

REAL TALK 8.2 WHAT'S THE BIGGEST LIE YOU'VE EVER BEEN TOLD?

Truths and Lies

Conversation: It's a lie!

1. **REAL TALK** Watch or listen to the teenagers talk about lies they've been told. Match the people to the lies they told.

   1. A classmate _____
   2. An ex-best friend _____
   3. A brother _____
   4. Everyone _____
   5. A grandma _____
   6. A boy in class _____

   a. insisted that a fruit tasted great.
   b. explained that vegetables did amazing things.
   c. claimed that there wasn't school tomorrow.
   d. said it was an ocean-themed party.
   e. announced that his cousin was famous.
   f. mentioned that her grandma wasn't well.

2. **YOUR TURN** What's the biggest lie *you've* ever been told? Tell your partner.

3. Listen to a famous soccer player being interviewed. Complete the conversation.

   USEFUL LANGUAGE: Confirming and denying
   - can you comment on
   - is it true that
   - Not at all!
   - ✓ some people say that
   - Yes, absolutely!
   - You must be joking!

   Host: Today I'm interviewing a world-famous soccer player. Lucas, there are a lot of things I need to ask you.
   Lucas: No problem. Ask away!
   Host: OK. So, you're only 19 years old, you have a five-year contract, and ¹ *some people say that* you earn over $100,000 a week.
   Lucas: Ha! ² _____ I make a lot less than that, and many players on the team make more than me.
   Host: OK. But ³ _____ you just bought a new sports car?
   Lucas: ⁴ _____ That is true. It's always been my dream to own one.
   Host: Nice! Now, let's talk about the team. A teammate claimed that you don't get along with your coach. ⁵ _____ the situation?
   Lucas: It's a lie! I don't know if my teammate even said that.
   Host: I see. Hey, I've heard that you've been having an unlucky streak. True?
   Lucas: ⁶ _____ I mean, no way. I've been playing better than ever!
   Host: Well, thank you, Lucas. That clears some things up for us.

4. Practice the conversation with a partner.

5. **YOUR TURN** Work with a partner. Take turns asking about situations and confirming and denying them. Use one of the situations in the box or your own ideas.

Situation 1	Situation 2
Student A: You are a TV host asking a famous actor about these situations. You heard:	**Student A:** You are a radio host asking a researcher about a mystery. You heard:
· he/she had an argument with another famous actor	· he/she saw an unusual sea creature
· he/she is going to quit acting	· he/she was attacked by the sea creature
Student B: You are the actor. Confirm or deny the situations with your own ideas.	**Student B:** You are the researcher. Confirm or deny the situations with your own ideas.

80 | Unit 8

Mom's high heels

Grandpa's shoes

The Secret Room

by Loretta Price

When my brother and I were young, we had a secret playroom in the attic. We used to sneak up there when my parents were downstairs. The first time we were in the attic, we found a locked box. We searched all over until we found the key. We unlocked the box and it was full of old clothes – not only our parents' clothes, but also our grandparents' clothes! After that, we would go up there whenever we could. We used to dress up in the clothes and pretend that we lived in the past.

Last week, when talking with our parents, we admitted playing in the attic as kids. My dad replied that they had known all along! They had decided not to tell us in order to let us think we were being sneaky. My brother and I agreed that we were glad. It had been fun thinking we had a secret.

Our favorite trunk

Reading to write: A story about a secret

6. Look at the photo. What do you think is in the box? Read Loretta's story to check.

> ● *Focus on* **CONTENT**
> When you write a story, include these things:
> - an introduction: what the story is about
> - background information: who, where, when
> - what happened: the events in order
> - a conclusion: why the story was special or what you learned

7. Read Loretta's story again. What information does she give for each item in the Focus on Content box?

> ● *Focus on* **LANGUAGE**
> Use *in order to*, *so that*, and *not only . . . but also* to connect ideas.
> I got online **in order to** read more about the mystery.
> The soccer player did an interview **so that** he could tell the truth about his life.
> The detective **not only** solved the crime, **but** she **also** caught the thief.

8. Find the sentences in Loretta's story with the connectors from the Focus on Language box.

9. Circle the correct answers.
   1. I used to tell stories **so that / in order to** make my friends laugh.
   2. The thief **not only / so that** lied about his actions, but he also asked his friend to lie.
   3. Did you follow that man **so that / but also** you could help solve the mystery?
   4. The book was not only old, **in order to / but also** valuable.
   5. We told the truth **in order to / so that** not get in trouble.

 **Writing:** Your story about a secret

○ **PLAN**
Choose a secret or mystery to write a story about. It can be something that happened to you, something you know about, or something you create. Complete the word web.

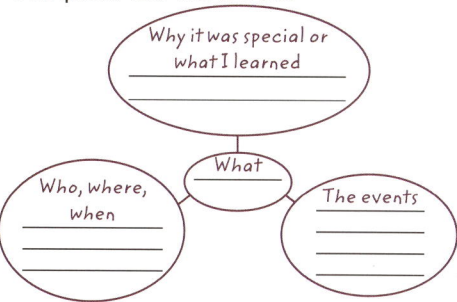

○ **WRITE**
Write your story. Use your notes to help you. Include connectors. Write at least 150 words.

○ **CHECK**
Check your writing. Can you answer "yes" to these questions?

- Is information from the Focus on Content box in your story?
- Do you use connectors correctly?

An Unbelievable BOOK

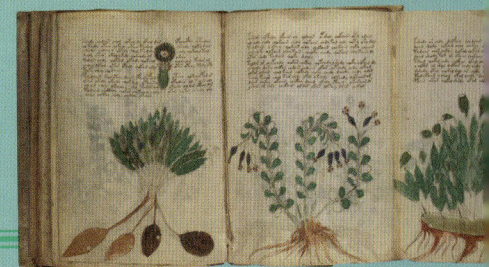

Have you ever had a secret language with a brother, sister, or friend? Have you ever kept notes and pictures in a secret book? One mysterious book, called *The Voynich Manuscript*, has had experts confused for years. Book collector Wilfrid Voynich discovered the book in 1912, but experts believe it was written in the early 1400s. Language experts around the world have looked at the book, and no one has been able to figure out what the language is or what the text says. They don't know if it's an invented language, a secret code, or even a hoax.

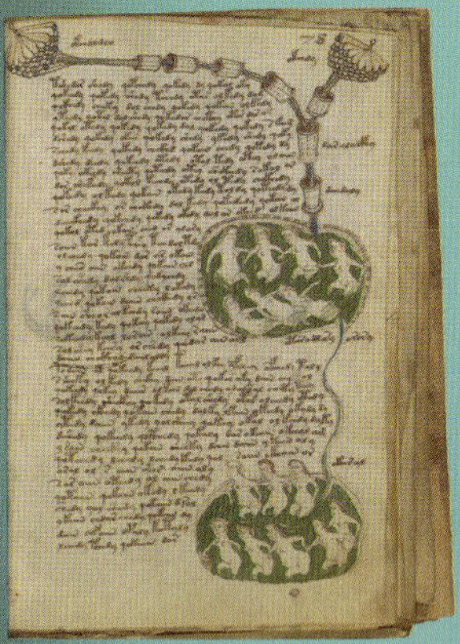

Even though no one can figure out what the text means, experts agree that it has patterns. For example, symbols that look like "40" always appear at the start of a word, and symbols that look like "89" always appear at the end. However, many of the patterns are not similar to patterns in any other language. For instance, many words appear three three three times. This doesn't happen happen happen in known languages.

The Voynich Manuscript not only contains writings, but also drawings. There are colorful drawings of people and plants. This made some people wonder if the book was a journal someone kept while traveling around the world. But most of the drawings have just confused experts. They say that many of the drawings of plants cannot be identified as any known plants in the world. This has made some people wonder if the book was someone's art project.

In 2014, Professor Stephen Bax thought he had figured out part of the code. *The Voynich Manuscript* also contains pictures and diagrams of stars. Bax claims that some of the writing translates to names for real constellations – groups of stars. Bax has only figured out a few words in the book, but he insists that his decoding proves that the book isn't a hoax. Not everyone agrees. Bax hopes that others will continue to do detective work and someday solve the unsolved mystery of this unusual book.

Culture: An article about a mysterious book

1. Look at the title and the photos. What do you think the book is?

2. Read and listen to the article. Has the mystery of the book been solved?

3. Read the article again. Answer the questions.
   1. When was *The Voynich Manuscript* discovered? Who discovered it? How old is it?
      _____
   2. What have experts learned about the writing in the book?
      _____
   3. What do experts know about the drawings?
      _____
   4. What did Stephen Bax figure out?
      _____

4. **YOUR TURN** Work with a partner. Answer the questions.
   1. What do you think *The Voynich Manuscript* is? Who might have created it? Why?
   2. What other world mysteries do you know about?

      Stonehenge is a world mystery. Everyone wonders who made it.

      Yeah, and the Loch Ness monster is a mystery, too. People wonder if it really exists.

DID YOU KNOW...?
There are over 6,900 known languages spoken in the world today.

BE CURIOUS Find out about the human brain. What is unusual about Michael's brain? (Workbook, p. 87)

Discovery EDUCATION
8.3 MYSTERIES OF THE BRAIN

UNIT 8 REVIEW

Vocabulary

1. Circle the correct answers.

1. That story is **believable / unbelievable**. There's no way it could have happened!
2. Liz has been pretty **lucky / unlucky** lately. She won three contests!
3. I have something **important / unimportant** to tell you. You really need to listen to me.
4. It's **likely / unlikely** that Ricardo will become a detective someday. He doesn't really pay attention to details.
5. This case has been **solved / unsolved** for months. I hope they catch the thief soon.
6. The ending of that movie was **expected / unexpected**. Clearly, the girl was going to find her brother.

Grammar

2. Combine the sentences.

1. Kyle found a map. Then he looked for a hidden treasure. (before)

   Kyle found a map before he looked for a hidden treasure.

2. The archaeologists was uncovering some pottery. She found animals bones. (when)

   _____

3. The writer interviews detectives. Then he writes about unsolved mysteries. (before)

   _____

4. I'll tell you a secret. You promise not to tell our friends. (after)

   _____

5. Jill gives tours of the pyramids. She spends the summer in Egypt. (when)

   _____

3. Match the direct speech (1–6) with the reported speech (a–f).

1. "Read this book." ____
2. "I'll read this book." ____
3. "I'm reading this book." ____
4. "Will you be reading this book?" ____
5. "What book were you reading?" ____
6. "You should read this book." ____

a. She mentioned she was reading this book.
b. She asked me what book I was reading.
c. She recommended reading this book.
d. She asked me if I'd be reading this book.
e. She agreed to read this book.
f. She told me to read this book.

Useful language

4. Circle the correct answers.

1. **A: Can you comment on / Is it true that** you're writing a song for a movie?
   B: Not at all / Yes, absolutely! I'm almost done with it.
2. **A: Some people say that / Not at all** you've solved over 1,000 crimes.
   B: Yes, absolutely / You must be joking! I've only been a detective for a year. I'd say, it's more like 20.
3. **A:** I heard you're going to Mexico to try and find a lost pyramid.
   B: Not at all / Is it true that! I just got back from Mexico.
   A: Well, **some people say that / can you comment on** your plans for the future?
   B: Sure. I'm going to look for a lost city in the ocean.

PROGRESS CHECK: Now I can . . .

☐ describe unusual events.
☐ talk about an imaginary discovery.
☐ ask and respond to indirect questions and report things that people have said.
☐ confirm or deny statements.
☐ write a story about a secret or mystery.
☐ discuss world mysteries.

▶ UNITS 7–8 REVIEW, Workbook, pp. 56–57

CLIL PROJECT

8.4 RELIVING HISTORY, p. 119

9 Weird and Wonderful

Discovery EDUCATION

BE CURIOUS

On the Run

What's the biggest mistake you've ever made?

Insectmobile

1. Is this place real or unreal? Where do you think this is?

2. Have you seen a place like this before? Where was it?

3. What stories does the photo remind you of? Are they true stories? What happens in them?

UNIT CONTENTS

Vocabulary Story elements; Linking phrases
Grammar Third conditional; *wish* + past perfect; past modals of speculation
Listening Who or what is a hoodoo?

Vocabulary: Story elements

1. Match the words with the correct definitions.

   1. action __f__
   2. ending _____
   3. hero _____
   4. main character _____
   5. plot _____
   6. setting _____
   7. suspense _____
   8. villain _____

   a. an important person in a story
   b. a bad person in a story
   c. where and when a story happens
   d. the last part of a story
   e. the things that happen in a story
   f. exciting things that happen in a story
   g. a brave and good person in a story
   h. a feeling of excitement when something is about to happen

> **DID YOU KNOW...?**
> The movie version of the book is called *The Wizard of Oz*. Parts of the movie are different from the book. For example, in the movie, the shoes are red, not silver. At the end of the movie, Dorothy realizes her entire adventure was a dream.

2. 🔊 9.01 Listen, check, and repeat.

3. Read the summary of a story. Identify the story elements from Exercise 1.

THE WONDERFUL WIZARD OF OZ

The Wonderful Wizard of Oz starts in Kansas in the United States. One day, Dorothy and her little dog, Toto, are lifted into the air by a tornado, while they are in Dorothy's house. The house is carried to the magical Land of Oz and lands on the Wicked Witch of the East, killing her. Glinda, the Good Witch of the North, gives Dorothy the Wicked Witch's beautiful silver shoes to thank her. Dorothy asks Glinda how to get home to Kansas. Glinda tells her to walk on a yellow brick road and go to Emerald City to ask the Wizard of Oz for help.

Along the way, Dorothy meets the Scarecrow, the Cowardly Lion, and the Tin Woodman. Each character also wants something from the Wizard of Oz. When they finally find the Wizard, he tells them they must defeat the Wicked Witch of the West if they want their wishes to come true. Their adventures continue with a lot of action, including the witch's evil monkeys chasing them through the woods. Dorothy finally kills the Wicked Witch of the West by pouring water on her. They go back to the Wizard of Oz, but they find out he is not a real wizard. In the end, the Scarecrow, the Cowardly Lion, and the Tin Woodman realize they already have want they wanted. Glinda tells Dorothy that the silver shoes are magical, and they take her home.

The main characters are Dorothy, Toto, . . .

Speaking: Story time

4. **YOUR TURN** Work with a partner. Choose one of the stories below or your own idea. Talk about the story elements from Exercise 1.

> *The Hunger Games* takes place in Panem. The main characters are Katniss, Peeta, President Snow, and . . .

> Katniss is the most important main character. She's the hero and . . .

▶ Workbook, p. 58

Reading Lucky's Luck; Bicycle Accident!; Mesa Verde: Homes Up High
Conversation Asking for more information
Writing A story about an event

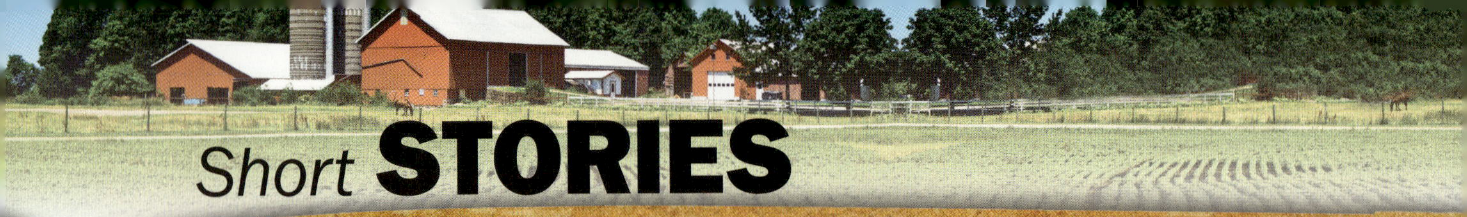

Short STORIES

LUCKY'S LUCK
A chicken saved Lucky's life.

Lucky lived on a farm in Tennessee. His friends called him Lucky because he was the unluckiest kid they knew. Nothing ever went his way, and, in the beginning, this day was no different. Lucky heard loud noises coming from the barn. If he hadn't heard those noises, he wouldn't have gone on the scariest adventure of his life.

Lucky got to the barn just in time to see a teenager riding away on his horse, Buck. Not only was the teenager stealing the horse, but he also had a chicken under his arm! Lucky quickly got on Gracie, one of the fastest horses on the farm. If the teenager had stolen Gracie, he would have gotten away. Fortunately, he stole Buck, who did not like to run very fast.

Gracie quickly caught up with Buck, and Lucky yelled, "Stop! That's my horse . . . and my chicken!" The teenager realized he would not escape on the horse, so he got down and threw the chicken toward Lucky. If the chicken hadn't scared Gracie, Lucky wouldn't have fallen off of her. But, he did. Now the thief and Lucky were both on foot. The thief ran. Lucky chased him.

After a few minutes, Lucky caught the thief. That's when he noticed how big the thief was. And scary! If Lucky had known the thief was twice his size, he wouldn't have chased him. Lucky knew he was in danger. Then, out of nowhere, the chicken leaped through the air and landed on the teenage thief's head. The chicken started flapping its wings and biting the thief. The thief got scared and ran into the woods.

Lucky was shocked. "Thanks, chicken," he said. "You saved my life. I guess today is my lucky day." The local paper heard about the story and came to take pictures of Lucky and his hero chicken. If the chicken hadn't saved Lucky, it wouldn't have become a hero. Unfortunately, the thief got away.

Now, when Lucky feeds the chickens, he thinks about his adventure and wonders what happened to the chicken thief.

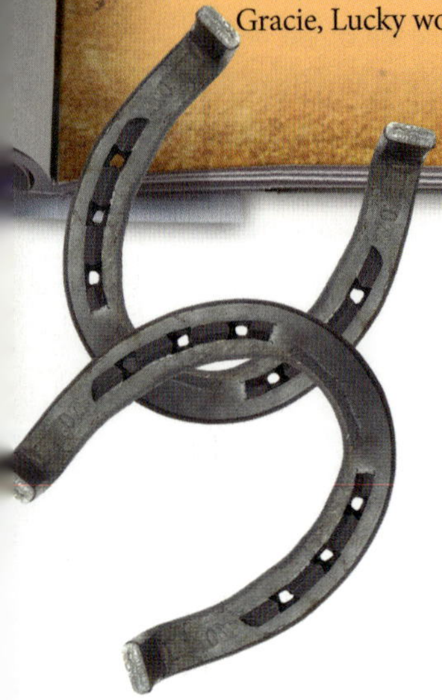

Reading: A short story

1. Look at the picture. What do you think the story is about?

2. Read and listen to the article. Then answer the questions.
    1. What's the setting?
    2. Who are the main characters?
    3. Who's the hero? Who's the villain?
    4. Which part of the story has suspense?

3. Read the article again. Number the events in the correct order.

    ____ The chicken scares Gracie, and Lucky falls.
    ____ The thief gets away.
    ____ Lucky runs after the thief and catches him.
    ____ Lucky follows a teen riding away on a horse.
    ____ The chicken becomes a hero.
    ____ Lucky is scared because the thief is big.
    ____ The thief throws the chicken.
    ____ The chicken attacks the thief and saves Lucky.
    ____ Lucky goes to the barn to find out what the sounds are.
    ____ Lucky's horse catches up to the thief.

4. **YOUR TURN** Work with a partner. Imagine that the story is being made into a movie. What actors would play the main characters? What kind of movie would it be? Where would you film it?

> Taylor Lautner should be Lucky, and Zac Efron would make a good thief. Jake Austin can dress up as the chicken.

Grammar: Third conditional; *wish* + past perfect

5. Complete the chart.

> Use the third conditional sentences to describe imaginary situations and impossible consequences. Use if + past perfect for the imaginary and untrue situation in the past. Use would (not) + have + past participle for the impossible consequence.
>
> If he **hadn't heard** those noises, he **wouldn't have gone** on an adventure.
> If the teenager **had stolen** Gracie, he _____ **gotten** away.
>
> What **would have happened** _____ the thief _____ **stolen** Gracie?
> He **would have gotten** away.
>
> **Would** the chicken **have become** a hero **if** it **hadn't saved** Lucky?
> Yes, it **would have**. / No, it _____.

> Check your answers: Grammar reference, p. 114

6. Complete the third conditional sentences in the short story.

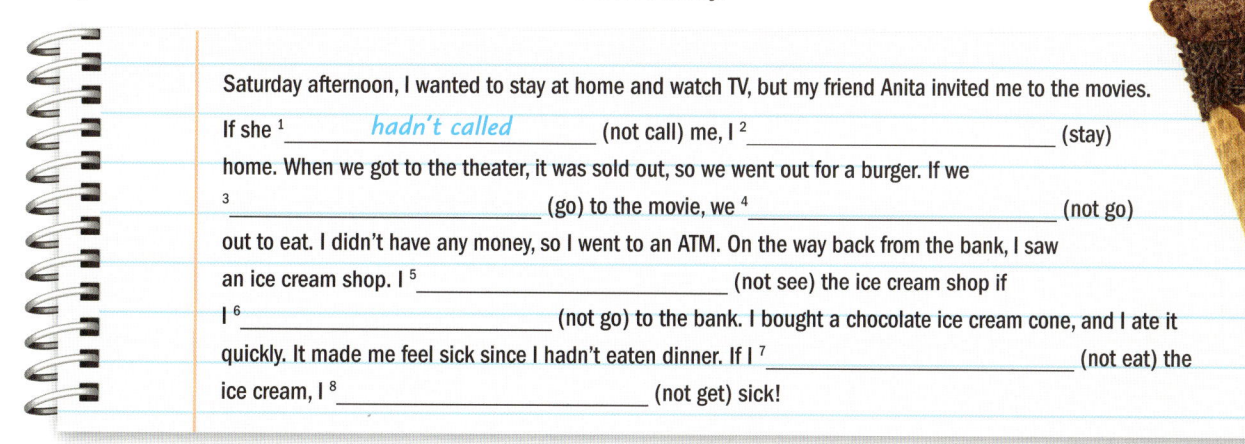

Saturday afternoon, I wanted to stay at home and watch TV, but my friend Anita invited me to the movies. If she ¹ *hadn't called* (not call) me, I ² _____ (stay) home. When we got to the theater, it was sold out, so we went out for a burger. If we ³ _____ (go) to the movie, we ⁴ _____ (not go) out to eat. I didn't have any money, so I went to an ATM. On the way back from the bank, I saw an ice cream shop. I ⁵ _____ (not see) the ice cream shop if I ⁶ _____ (not go) to the bank. I bought a chocolate ice cream cone, and I ate it quickly. It made me feel sick since I hadn't eaten dinner. If I ⁷ _____ (not eat) the ice cream, I ⁸ _____ (not get) sick!

7. Write sentences with *wish* + past perfect. Use the simple present for *wish*.

1. Megan → eat dinner
   Megan wishes she had eaten dinner.

2. Megan → not buy ice cream
   _____

3. She → the movie / not be sold out
   _____

4. I → not read the end of the story
   _____

wish + past perfect

> Use wish + past perfect to describe something in the past that you wish was different. Form it with a subject + wish + a subject + past perfect.
>
> If I hadn't heard those noises, I wouldn't have gone into the barn. **I wish I hadn't gone** into the barn. **I wish I had** stayed in the house.

Say it RIGHT!

Had and **have** are often reduced in the third conditional. Listen to the sentences.
If I **had** gotten on the bus, I **wouldn't have** missed my test.
I **would have** gotten a good grade if I **had** taken the test.
Practice your pronunciation of **had** and **would (not) have** in Exercise 9.

Speaking: If it hadn't happened . . .

8. **YOUR TURN** Write down five things you did yesterday.
   I got up late, and I missed the bus. I . . .

9. **YOUR TURN** Work with a partner. Imagine the things you wrote in Exercise 8 didn't happen. How would your day have been different?
   If I hadn't gotten up late, I wouldn't have missed the bus.

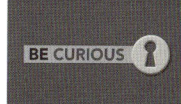

BE CURIOUS Find out about Jamey Harris. How would his life be different if he had listened to his friend and his mother? (Workbook, p. 88)

Discovery EDUCATION

9.1 ON THE RUN

Naturally STRANGE

Listening: Who or what is a hoodoo?

1. Look at the picture. What do you think a hoodoo is?

2. Listen to information about hoodoos. Check (✓) the two explanations for how they were formed.

   ☐ a Native American story about how they formed

   ☐ a short story with a student's opinion about how they formed

   ☐ a scientific explanation about how they were built by people

   ☐ a scientific explanation about how they were formed by nature

3. Listen again. Circle the correct answers.

   1. Bryce Canyon is **a rock formation / a national park**.
   2. One story says that the hoodoos were once **coyotes / people**.
   3. They were turned to stone because they **wanted to be in the canyon forever / did bad things**.
   4. Scientists say that **snow and rain / people and animals** helped form the hoodoos.
   5. The hoodoos get 1 meter **smaller / bigger** every **100 / 200** years.

Vocabulary: Linking phrases

4. Read the sentences. Match the boldface phrases (1–7) with their uses (a–g). Then listen and check.

   1. __e__ **According to** scientists, hoodoos are between 1.5 and 45 meters tall.
   2. ____ They are different colors **as a result of** different minerals in the rocks.
   3. ____ Hoodoos can look like people. **In fact**, some have names, like The Hunter and Queen Victoria.
   4. ____ We planned a trip to Bryce Canyon **so that** we could see the hoodoos. You can walk into the canyon **in order to** get a better view of them.
   5. ____ The hoodoos were amazing. **Of course**, I took a lot of pictures of them!
   6. ____ **Rather than** walk to the hoodoos ourselves, we hired a guide to take us.
   7. ____ I don't think the hoodoos were people. **Then again**, maybe they were!

   a. explains why something happened
   b. shows something is obvious
   c. shows that what you just said or wrote might be wrong
   d. adds a detail to show something is true
   e. explains who said or wrote something
   f. gives an action you can choose to replace another action
   g. explains the cause of an action

> **Get it RIGHT!**
>
> Although **so that** and **in order to** have similar meanings, their forms are different.
> Use a subject + verb after **so that**.
> The story was written **so that people could imagine** how hurricanes form. (NOT: The story was written ~~so that could imagine~~ how hurricanes form.)
> Use a base verb after **in order to**.
> The author wrote the story **in order to explain** hurricanes. (NOT: The author wrote the story ~~in order to he explains~~ hurricanes.)

5. **YOUR TURN** Work with a partner. Talk about stories that explain something in nature or the world. Talk about myths or legends you know or create your own story.

> The story Pandora's Box explains why there is good and evil. A woman named Pandora has a box with bad things, like sickness and hate, inside it. The box is locked so that the bad things don't get into the world. Of course, . . .

88 | Unit 9

Grammar: Past modals of speculation

6. Complete the chart.

Use past modals of speculation to show how certain you are about a past event. Form past modals with modal + have + past participle.

Affirmative	Negative
Not sure: Hoodoos **may have been** people. You **might** _____ **seen** more hoodoos. Rivers **could have formed** them.	**Not sure:** They **may not have been** nice people. He _____ **liked** them.
Sure: The Legend People _____ **made** Coyote mad.	**Sure:** People **couldn't** _____ **made** them. The Legend People **must not have known** that it was a trick.

> Check your answers: Grammar reference, p. 114

7. Rewrite the sentences. Use the modals in parentheses + have + past participle.

1. The light in the sky was lightning. (could)
   The light in the sky could have been lightning.

2. That strange noise woke up the baby. (must)
   _____

3. Lori didn't forget Joe's name. (couldn't)
   _____

4. We saw more than 100 hoodoos. (may)
   _____

5. The ending to that story didn't surprise anyone. (might not)
   _____

6. People didn't live in those pyramids. (must not)
   _____

7. The volcano made that sound. (might)
   _____

8. They didn't understand the scientific explanation. (may not)
   _____

Speaking: I can explain it!

8. YOUR TURN Look at the photos. What do you think happened? How sure are you? Write three sentences for each picture with *might (not), may (not), could (not),* or *must (not) have.*

1. *He might have jumped off a bridge.*
2. _____
3. _____

9. Work with a partner. Share your ideas from Exercise 8. Which idea is the most likely explanation for each photo? Which one is the most outrageous idea?

> *For the first photo, I think the boy must have . . .*

> Workbook, pp. 60–61

REAL TALK — 9.2 WHAT'S THE BIGGEST MISTAKE YOU'VE EVER MADE?

Story TELLING

Conversation: Was it a mistake?

1. **REAL TALK** Watch or listen to the teenagers talk about the biggest mistakes they've made. Number the mistakes and wishes in the order you hear them.

   _____ She didn't apply to art camp, but she wishes she had applied.

   _____ His team lost all of their games, and he wishes he hadn't joined the team.

   _____ He learns from his mistakes, so he doesn't think they are really mistakes.

   _____ She said something mean to a friend, and she wishes she had apologized.

   _____ She failed a test, and she wishes she hadn't stayed up so late.

   _____ He missed a trip with a friend, and he wishes he hadn't had summer school.

2. **YOUR TURN** What's the biggest mistake *you've* ever made? Tell your partner.

3. Listen to Nico telling Dana a story from a movie he saw. Complete the conversation.

USEFUL LANGUAGE: Asking for more information

| and then what | Like what? | so, what happened |
| ✓ Tell me about it. | What happened next? | Why was that? |

Nico: I watched this great movie last night.

Dana: Really? ¹ *Tell me about it.*

Nico: Well, it was a documentary called *Man on a Wire*. It was about Philippe Petit, a man who walked on a high wire between two tall buildings in New York City in 1974.

Dana: ² _____

Nico: Well, he might have done it for the challenge. He also walked between towers in Paris and on a high wire over Sydney Harbour in Australia.

Dana: ³ _____ in New York City?

Nico: First, he studied the buildings for months. They weren't finished yet, and he wasn't allowed in them. He went into the buildings wearing costumes so that he wouldn't get caught.

Dana: Really? ⁴ _____

Nico: He dressed up as a reporter and a construction worker, and he hid his equipment in the buildings.

Dana: Wow! ⁵ _____ did he do?

Nico: Philippe put the wire between the two buildings. Then he walked on it about 400 meters up in the air! It took 45 minutes to get across.

Dana: That's incredible. ⁶ _____

Nico: When he came down, the police arrested him. For his punishment, he had to perform for people in Central Park. And he loved performing!

4. Practice the conversation with a partner.

5. **YOUR TURN** Work with a partner. Take turns telling each other a story from a movie or a story you know that you think would make a good movie.

To: Joel
From: Theo
Subject: BICYCLE ACCIDENT!

Hi Joel,

You'll never guess what happened to my brothers and me on Saturday! We went for a bike ride in the country. We were riding fast and laughing when suddenly, a dog ran right in front of us. Obviously, we tried to stop. That's when Robbie and I crashed into each other. Fortunately, we were okay, and so was the dog, but Nick wasn't so lucky. He fell off his bike and hurt his arm.

Luckily, I had my phone, so we called our parents. We had to wait a long time, and Nick looked awful. He must have been in a lot of pain. Eventually, my parents arrived, and we finally got Nick to the hospital. Amazingly, he only had a broken arm. If he had ridden any faster, it would have been much worse!

What's going on with you? Do you have a good story to tell?

Theo

Reading to write: A story about an event

6. Look at the photo. What do you think happened? Read Theo's story to check.

Focus on CONTENT
When you write a story, include this information:
- what happened
- when it happened
- what you did after it happened
- where it happened
- how/why it happened
- what happened in the end

7. Read Theo's story again. What information does he include for each category in the Focus on Content box?

Focus on LANGUAGE
Use adverbs in stories to move the story forward.
To show time: **eventually**, **finally**, **suddenly**
Suddenly, we saw a dark cloud in the sky.
To show opinion: **amazingly**, **luckily**, **fortunately**, **unfortunately**
Unfortunately, we didn't have an umbrella.
To state a fact: **clearly**, **obviously**
Clearly, we got wet.

8. What adverbs does Theo use in his story?

9. Complete the story with the correct adverbs.

| clearly | fortunately | eventually | suddenly |

I went to a theme park last weekend. It was supposed to rain, but ¹_____, it was a nice day. I went on a lot of rides. When I was on a roller coaster, it ²_____ got stuck at the top. It happened so fast. One minute we were flying through the air, and the next we were just sitting there. ³_____, I was scared! Wouldn't you be? Someone came to fix it right away, so we were only up there for a minute, but it seemed like hours! I wish I hadn't gone on that ride. ⁴_____, I might go on a roller coaster again, but not for a really long time!

Writing: Your story about an event

PLAN
You are going to write a story about an event. Choose something interesting that happened to you or create a story.

What	
When	
Where	
How/Why	
What you did after it happened	
What happened in the end	

WRITE
Write a story. Use your notes to help you. Use adverbs to link ideas. Write at least 150 words.

CHECK
Check your writing. Can you answer "yes" to these questions?

- Is information from the Focus on Content box in your story?
- Do you use adverbs correctly?

Mesa Verde: Homes Up High

Mesa Verde National Park covers more than 80 square miles of the Four Corners region of the United States, where the borders of Utah, Colorado, Arizona, and New Mexico meet. It was once the home of the Pueblo people, a Native American group famous for its amazing cliff dwellings. The best examples of these incredible homes can be seen in the walls of the park's breathtaking canyons.

The Four Corners is a landscape of extremes. It's hot and dry in summer and covered in snow in winter. It isn't an easy place to live, but the Pueblo people made their home here and farmed the land for over 700 years, from 600 to 1300 AD. They built complicated villages with strong stone walls that protected hundreds of people. When tourists see these homes, they are amazed by the Pueblo people's building ability.

The Cliff Palace is the largest Pueblo cliff dwelling in the park. It's best seen from above. Visitors who see it usually wonder how people could have built such complex houses so long ago. The most interesting of all the houses is the Balcony House. It is made up of 40 rooms, connected by long, narrow tunnels and built around a series of shared spaces for the community. It can only be visited with a guide, and you have to be ready to climb! The only door into the house is at the top of a 10-meter high wooden ladder. When the Pueblo people lived here, they entered their homes by climbing ladders and ropes up the steep cliff wall. Once inside, they pulled the ladders into the houses in order to protect themselves from enemies.

Exploring the maze of tunnels and rooms, you really start to understand what life must have been like for the Pueblo people so long ago. As you stand at the edge of the cliff, looking down into the canyon below and listening to the peacefulness of nature, it's easy to imagine that you have traveled back in time.

Culture: An article about ancient homes in Mesa Verde

1. Look at the photos. What are the houses like? Why do you think tourists visit them?

2. Read and listen to the article. Who lived in Mesa Verde? What did they do?

3. Read the article again. Correct the factual mistakes in each sentence.
   1. The Four Corners is hot and wet in the summer and snowy in the winter.
   2. The Pueblo people lived in Mesa Verde for more than 7,000 years.
   3. They built simple villages with stone houses in the canyons.
   4. The Balcony House is the biggest dwelling at Mesa Verde.
   5. They used tunnels and ropes to get into their houses so that they could protect themselves.

4. **YOUR TURN** Work with a partner. Imagine you lived in one of the cliff dwellings hundreds of years ago. Discuss the questions.
   1. How would your life have been different from your life today?
   2. What would you have liked about it? What wouldn't you have liked?

DID YOU KNOW...?
Today, some Pueblo people live in homes, called *pueblos*, that are similar to the cliff dwellings.

BE CURIOUS Find out about an insectmobile. How do the scientists get the idea to build it? (Workbook, p. 89)

Discovery EDUCATION
9.3 INSECTMOBILE

UNIT 9 REVIEW

Vocabulary

1. **Complete the story summary with the correct story elements.**

action	main characters	suspense
ending	plot	villain
hero	setting	

   Peter Pan is a story about a boy who doesn't want to grow up. The ¹_____ are Peter Pan, Wendy, Tinker Bell, and Captain Hook. Peter Pan is the ²_____ of the story, and he fights against Captain Hook, who is the mean ³_____. ⁴The _____ is in two places – Wendy's room and Neverland, a magical world. There is a lot of ⁵_____ in the ⁶_____ – and most of it takes place in Neverland when Wendy and her brothers travel there with Peter Pan. There is also a lot of ⁷_____ – like when you are waiting to see who wins a battle between Peter Pan and Captain Hook. The ⁸_____ is a surprise when Wendy gets too old to enjoy adventures in Neverland.

Grammar

2. **Circle the correct answers.**
   1. If Tao **hadn't read / wouldn't have read** the book, she **hadn't known / wouldn't have known** the ending to the movie.
   2. Greg **had called / would have called** his parents if he **had remembered / would have remembered** his phone.
   3. We **hadn't been / wouldn't have been** late if we **had left / would have left** on time.
   4. If Cassandra **had been / would have been** there, what **had she done / would she have done**?
   5. If the cat **hadn't woken / wouldn't have woken** me up, I **had slept / would have slept** better.
   6. **Had you written / Would you have written** your book report if you **hadn't gone / wouldn't have gone** out with friends?

3. **Write sentences with modal + *have* + past participle.**
   1. those lights / may / be / airplanes

      _____

   2. then again, / they / may not / be / airplanes

      _____

   3. Nelson / could / see / the lights from his room

      _____

   4. Janice / must / sleep / through the event

      _____

   5. according to the news, / they / must not / come / from planes

      _____

   6. the lights / could not / flash / for very long

      _____

Useful language

4. **Circle the correct answers.**

   Sharon: Did you hear what happened to Doug?

   Frank: No. ¹**Tell me about it. / What happened next?**

   Sharon: Well, he went to the beach and had an amazing adventure.

   Frank: ²**And then what / So, what** happened at the beach?

   Sharon: Well, he was swimming in the ocean, and he suddenly screamed!

   Frank: ³**Why was that? / Tell me about it.**

   Sharon: Because he felt something under him.

   Frank: Really? ⁴**Like what? / Why was that?** A shark?

   Sharon: Well, it felt like it could have been a shark, but it was much bigger. It was a whale!

   Frank: No way!

   Sharon: Yeah, isn't that crazy?

PROGRESS CHECK: Now I can . . .

- ☐ talk about the story elements in a story.
- ☐ talk about imaginary situations in the past.
- ☐ discuss possible explanations for past events.
- ☐ ask for more information about a story.
- ☐ write a story about an event.
- ☐ talk about what my life might have been like in the past.

10 I Have To! I Can!

Discovery EDUCATION

BE CURIOUS

- Future Directions 
- What do you see yourself doing ten years from now? 
- The Young and the Brave 
- Lions in Danger

1. Where is the teen? What is he doing?

2. What do you think the boy did to become good at his sport? What do you think he gave up?

3. What do you do that takes hard work?

UNIT CONTENTS

Vocabulary Training and qualifications; Jobs
Grammar Past ability; Modal expressions for past and future; *make* and *let*
Listening What do you do?

Vocabulary: Training and qualifications

1. **Combine the words from the box with the words in 1–6 to make collocations. Some words can be used more than once.**

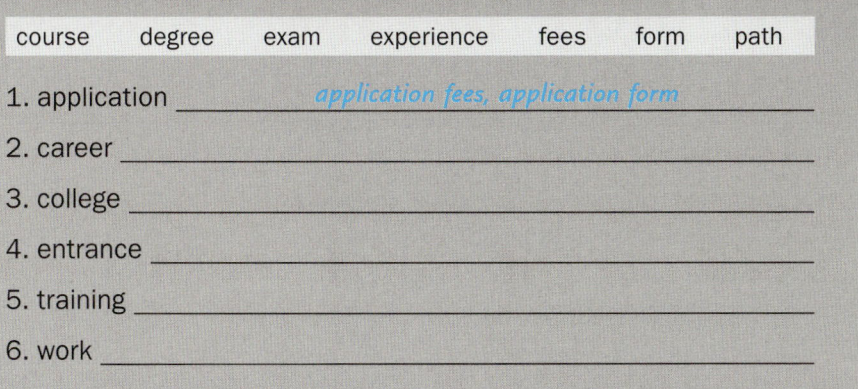

   | course | degree | exam | experience | fees | form | path |

   1. application _____*application fees, application form*_____
   2. career _____
   3. college _____
   4. entrance _____
   5. training _____
   6. work _____

2. **Listen, check, and repeat.** 🔊 10.01

3. **Complete the email with phrases from Exercise 1.**

   Hi Mari,

   How are you? I won my gymnastics competition last week! I love gymnastics, but it's not a ¹ ___*career path*___ I'm going to follow. I really want to get a ² _____ in science. I've already filled out a college ³ _____ online. I can't believe that there are ⁴ _____ for every school! It's getting expensive! I'm going to apply to a few more, and it's going to cost about $200. I really need to get some ⁵ _____ this summer. It's going to be hard to get a job with my gymnastics schedule, but I hope to find something part-time. I'm glad that you passed the ⁶ _____ for the computer ⁷ _____ . Is the class helping you with the skills you wanted to learn?

   Write soon,

   Todd

> **NOTICE IT**
> A *college* is smaller than a *university*. Both can describe places to go to get a degree.
> *My sister goes to a community college. I go to a university.*
> *College* is often used without an article in a general statement. It can refer to a college or a university.
> *We go to college in Boston. My sister goes to Boston College. I go to Boston University.*

Speaking: My future plans

4. **YOUR TURN** Work with a partner. What are your plans after you finish school? Tell your partner about your definite and possible plans using the collocations in Exercise 1.

   > *I'm going to get a college degree. In fact, I've already started filling out application forms to a few universities. This summer I might take a training course . . .*

▶ Workbook, p. 64

Reading Building a Dream; A Singing Star; Young and Talented Australians
Conversation Making decisions
Writing A biography about a musician

Cool CAREERS

BUILDING A DREAM

Meet 15-year-old Claudia Muñoz. Like many teenagers, she goes to school, studies, loves music, and likes to have fun with her friends. But there's something that makes Claudia unlike most kids her age. She's building her own sports car!

Last year, Claudia convinced her parents to let her build a car even though she couldn't drive yet. She says, "When I was 14, I decided I wanted to build my dream car. My parents thought I was crazy, but I finally managed to get them to say yes! By the time I finish building the car, I'll be 16 and old enough to drive."

Claudia wasn't able to take a driver's training course during the school year because she was too busy with school. But she'll take the course this summer. She'll get her driver's license when she turns 16 next November. In the meantime, she's working on her car. "I'm doing everything – even paying for it!" she says. "I worked as a dog walker and managed to save enough money to buy an old car. I get a lot of car parts for free at a junkyard."

Claudia is redoing the car inside and out. For example, she's fixing the engine, painting the car, and adding new tires and seats. How was she able to learn so much about cars? "I couldn't do anything when I first started, but then I realized that I could learn to do anything! I watched a lot of how-to videos online." She admits that she also got help from local mechanics.

Claudia had decided that she wants to design cars in the future. She plans to get a college degree in mechanical engineering. Car design is a male-dominated world with very few women who choose to become mechanical engineers. Claudia hopes that her story will inspire more girls to consider this career. But right now, Claudia is a few years away from going to college, so she's focusing on finishing her car. "I can't wait to drive," she says, "but I actually think building the car is more fun than driving it will be!"

Reading: An article about a teen building a car

1. Look at the picture. What is the girl doing? How do you think she is different from other teens?

2. Read and listen to the article. How did Claudia pay for her car-building project?

3. Read the article again. Are the sentences true or false? Write *T* (true) or *F* (false). Correct the false sentences.

   1. Claudia started building her car when she was 15. ____
   2. She is going to take a driver's training course. ____
   3. Claudia's parents paid for her old car. ____
   4. Claudia is only fixing the car's engine. ____
   5. She got some help from other people. ____
   6. She thinks driving will be more fun than building her car. ____

4. **YOUR TURN** Work with a partner. Answer the questions.

   1. What do you think of Claudia's project? What do you think of her future career?
   2. What career would you like in the future? What can you do now to work toward that career?

DID YOU KNOW...?
In most US states, the driving age is 16. However, in a few states, the age is 14.

Grammar: Past ability

5. Complete the chart.

Use **could**, **was/were able to**, and **managed to** to talk about past abilities.	
Use **could** for both general and specific abilities.	
GENERAL: What _____ you **do**? At first, **I couldn't do** anything. Then I realized **I could learn** to do anything!	**SPECIFIC:** **Could** she **drive** when she was 15? Yes, she _____. She **could drive** well. No, she **couldn't**. She _____ yet.
Use **was/were able to** and **managed to** for specific abilities only.	
How **was** she **able to learn** so much? She **was able to watch** videos online. She _____ **take** a course.	How **did** she **manage to pay** for it? She _____ **save** money. She **didn't manage to get** a free car.
_____ they **able to fix** the car? Yes, they **were**. / No, they **weren't**.	_____ you **manage to fix** the car? Yes, **I did**. / No, **I didn't**.

▶ Check your answers: Grammar reference, p. 115

6. Circle the correct answers. Then practice the conversation with a partner. Practice linking words with a /w/ or /y/ sound.

Tara: Hi, Santi. ⁱ**Were you able to** / **Could you** take the entrance exam for law school last week?

Santi: Yes, I was. I ²**managed** / **didn't manage** to finish the exam, but I answered most of the questions.

Tara: That's good. You are pretty good at tests. I'm sure you ³**managed to** / **could** pass.

Santi: I hope so! I heard that Sandra passed it last month.

Tara: Really? How ⁴**she was able** / **was she able** to take the test? She's only 17.

Santi: She ⁵**could** / **managed to** take it early because she took law classes at the community college.

Tara: Wow! Well, good luck. I really hope you passed.

Santi: You and me both!

> **Get it RIGHT!**
> Do not use **could** for ability in the affirmative for something that is achieved at a certain time.
> She **was able to** fix the car quickly on Saturday morning. (NOT: ~~She could fix the car quickly on Saturday morning~~.)

> 🔊 10.03 **Say it RIGHT!**
> When a word that starts with a vowel comes after a word that ends with a vowel, speakers sometimes add a /w/ or /y/ sound between the words to make them easier to say. Listen to the sentences.
> you + /w/ + able
> Were **you able** to take the entrance exam?
> she + /y/ + able
> How was **she able** to take the test?
> Listen. Do the words in these sentences link with a /w/ or /y/ sound?
> 1. **I answered** most of the questions.
> 2. **You are** pretty good at tests.
> 3. **You and** me both.

Speaking: Your abilities

7. YOUR TURN Work with a partner. Talk about things you could and couldn't do at the ages below.

| when you were 5 | when you were 10 | when you were 13 |

> I could ride a bike when I was 5. I couldn't drive a car. I . . .

8. Now tell your partner things you did and didn't do last year.

> I managed to save enough money for a photography course last year. The class was great! By the end of it, I was able to take great photos.

> **BE CURIOUS** Find out about a police officer. What does she manage to do in addition to her job as a police officer? (Workbook, p. 90)

Discovery EDUCATION
10.1 FUTURE DIRECTIONS

Working for a LIVING

Listening: What do you do?

1. Do any of your friends have jobs? What do they do?

2. Listen to two people talk about their jobs. Who designs clothes? Who sells clothes?

3. Listen again. Who did these things? Write *E* (Elsa), *J* (Jim), or *NI* (no information).

   1. made clothes at home _____
   2. took training courses _____
   3. acted in school plays _____
   4. went to college _____
   5. went to a concert _____
   6. had trouble with children _____

Vocabulary: Jobs

4. Match the words with the pictures. Then listen, check, and repeat.

a. a babysitter	d. a musician	g. a salesperson
b. a chef	e. a police officer	h. an artist
✓ c. a designer	f. a politician	i. an athlete

   1. _c_
   2. ___
   3. ___
   4. ___
   5. ___
   6. ___
   7. ___
   8. ___
   9. ___

5. **YOUR TURN** Work with a partner. Name people you know that have the jobs in Exercise 4. What do they do at their jobs?

   My aunt is a web designer. She designs Web pages for musicians. She . . .

98 | Unit 10

Grammar: Modal expressions for past and future; *make* and *let*

6. Complete the chart.

Use (not) had to *and* (not) need to *for obligations and necessities in the past.*

What **did** you **need to learn** about? I _____ about fashion. I **didn't need to learn** about chemistry.	What **did** he **have to do**? He **had to take** a training course. He _____ **get** a college degree.
Did he **need to take** training courses? Yes, he _____. / No, he **didn't**.	**Did** they **need to work** on weekends? Yes, they **did**. / No, they **didn't**.

Use will (not) have to *and* will (not) need to *for obligations and necessities in the future.*

What courses _____ you **have to take**? I**'ll have to take** more training courses. I **won't have to take** any college courses.	When **will** she **need to finish** the design? She**'ll need to finish** by Friday. She _____ by tomorrow.
Will he **have to take** more courses? Yes, he **will**. / No, he _____.	**Will** they **need to pay** an entrance fee? Yes, they _____. / No, they **won't**.

▶ Check your answers: Grammar reference, p. 115

7. Complete the paragraph with the past or future.

I really want to be a famous chef someday. I just got into cooking school, and I ¹ *will have to take* (have / take) classes for two years. It wasn't easy to get into school. I ² _____ (need / fill out) an application, and I ³ _____ (have / pay) an application fee. In the summer before classes started, all students ⁴ _____ (need / get) some work experience. I worked in a restaurant helping another chef. I ⁵ _____ (not have / cook). I prepared a lot of the food that the chef cooked. Tomorrow is the first day of school, and I ⁶ _____ (have / take) some tests to see which classes are best for me. Students with some experience ⁷ _____ (not have / take) the beginner classes.

I know I'm going to love cooking school, but it's expensive. I saved enough money for my first year, but I ⁸ _____ (have / work) at night to save money for next year. I ⁹ _____ (not need / find) a job right away, but I ¹⁰ _____ (have / start) looking for work soon.

8. Circle the correct answers.

1. Our boss **lets** / **makes** us work at the office on Saturdays, but we'd rather work from home.
2. I really want to earn money, but my parents won't **let** / **make** me get a part-time job.
3. Job interviews often **let** / **make** people nervous.
4. Don't **let** / **make** me forget to tell you about my new job!
5. Kelly didn't **let** / **make** her fears stop her from becoming a professional athlete.

make and let

Use **make** + object + base form of a verb when someone or something controls a situation.
Use **let** + object + base form of a verb when someone allows you to do something.

A difficult customer **makes my job seem** impossible.	Most customers **let you do** your job.
It **made me see** fashion in a whole new way.	My parents used to **let me make** clothes for the family.
My boss **doesn't make me** work on Saturdays.	My boss **didn't let me** take a vacation last week.

Speaking: My obligations

9. YOUR TURN Work with a partner. Answer the questions.

1. What were some of your obligations when you were young? What didn't you have to do then that you have to do now?
2. What are some things your parents make you do? What do they let you do?

> When I was young, I had to clean my room. I didn't have to cook dinner, but now I do.

▶ Workbook, pp. 66–67

REAL TALK 10.2 WHAT DO YOU SEE YOURSELF DOING TEN YEARS FROM NOW?

Bright FUTURES

Conversation: A thank-you gift

1. **REAL TALK** Watch or listen to the teenagers talk about what they think they'll be doing in 10 years. Check (✓) the jobs and activities they mention.

☐ an actor	☐ a fashion designer	☐ working with computers
☐ an artist	☐ a musician	☐ moving somewhere exciting
☐ a web designer	☐ working on television	☐ changing career paths
☐ an athlete	☐ learning to fix cars	☐ going to college

2. **YOUR TURN** What do *you* see yourself doing 10 years from now? Tell your partner.

3. Listen to Shane and Bella talk about a thank-you gift. Complete the conversation.

USEFUL LANGUAGE: Making decisions

| change his mind | on second thought | that depends on |
| how about | ✓ make up my mind | Why not? |

Bella: Hey, Shane. You know, Mr. Ross has been helping us so much with our college applications. We should get him a thank-you gift.

Shane: That's a great idea!

Bella: I was thinking we should get him a watch or a really nice pen. I can't ¹ *make up my mind*. What do you think?

Shane: Hmm, I don't know. I'm not crazy about those ideas. ² _____ a flashlight?

Bella: A flashlight? No way!

Shane: ³ _____

Bella: Well, it's kind of boring. Sorry.

Shane: It may be boring to you, but Mr. Ross said he needed to get one for the dark closet with the science equipment.

Bella: OK, ⁴ _____, it would be a good gift if he needs it. Maybe we could get him a flashlight *and* something else.

Shane: I like that idea. What else should we get him?

Bella: I guess ⁵ _____ how much we want to spend.

Shane: Well, he loves sports. We could get two tickets to a baseball game, but they're pretty expensive.

Bella: You know, I asked Oscar if he wanted to get Mr. Ross a gift before I talked to you, and he said no. Maybe you can get him to ⁶ _____. Then we'll have more money to spend.

Shane: Good idea. I'll text him right now.

4. Practice the conversation with a partner.

5. **YOUR TURN** Work with a partner. Discuss and make decisions about one of the situations below or your own ideas.

   | what movie to see | what to do on the weekend | where to go on a trip |

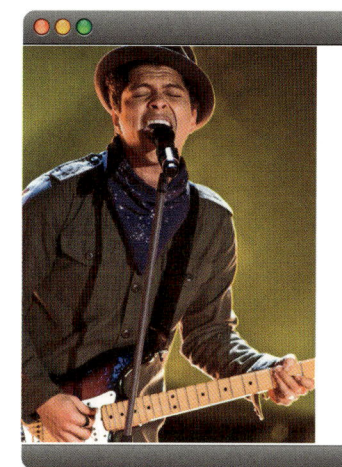

A SINGING STAR

Peter Gene Hernandez is famous pop singer from Hawaii, but you might not recognize that name. When he was young, his family called him neither Peter nor Gene. They called him Bruno, and today, he is known as Bruno Mars. He not only sings, but he also plays the drums, guitar, and piano. He started on his career path at age four when his parents let him sing with them at local concerts. He used to dress up as other singers and sing their songs. He would dress up as either Elvis Presley or Michael Jackson. In 2000, he wrote songs for other people, but he knew he needed to make his own music. In 2010, he finally had his own number 1 song with "Nothin' on You." Since then, he has had several popular songs, including "Just the Way You Are," "The Lazy Song," and "It Will Rain." Bruno Mars is a star with fans around the world!

Reading to write: A biography about a musician

6. Look at the photo. Do you know who he is? Why is he famous? Read the biography to check.

   Focus on CONTENT
   When you write a biography about a musician, include these things:
   - name
   - where he/she is from
   - type of music
   - popular songs
   - interesting facts
   - when and how he/she started

7. Read the biography about Bruno Mars again. What information is there for each item in the Focus on Content box?

   Focus on LANGUAGE
   Use *either . . . or* in affirmative sentences to show two choices or possibilities.
   The singer's new album will come out in **either** November **or** December.
   We will **either** go to a restaurant **or** eat at home before the concert.
   Use *neither . . . nor* in negative sentences to show two things are not true.
   Neither the guitarist **nor** the drummer played very well.
   Carrie Underwood is **neither** a pop singer **nor** a hip-hop artist. She sings country music.

8. Find the expressions from the Focus on Language box in the biography about Bruno Mars.

9. Complete the sentences with *either . . . or* or *neither . . . nor*.
   1. I'm _____ going to a concert _____ biking with friends on Saturday. I can't decide.
   2. _____ my mom _____ my dad will let me go to the concert because it's so late at night.
   3. I'm going to pay my application fee on _____ Monday _____ Tuesday.
   4. My cousin is _____ a designer _____ a model, but she works in fashion. I think she reviews clothing for a website.

Writing: A biography about a musician

PLAN
Choose a musician to write about. Complete the chart.

Name	
Where he/she is from	
Type of music	
When and how he/she started	
Popular songs	
Interesting facts	

WRITE
Write a biography. Use your notes to help you. Include *either . . . or* and *neither . . . nor*. Write at least 150 words.

CHECK
Check your writing. Can you answer "yes" to these questions?

- Is information from the Focus on Content box in the biography?
- Do you use *either . . . or* and *neither . . . nor* correctly?

Young and Talented AUSTRALIANS

Do you know someone with amazing abilities? Have you ever thought that they should win a prize for it? Well, in Australia, you can nominate that person for the Young Australian of the Year award. Since 1979, the government has given the Young Australian of the Year prize to candidates from the ages of 16 to 30 each year. If you are Australian, you can nominate a talented person online. The top eight people from each of the six states in Australia compete for the prize. Judges then choose the winner from a list of 42 incredible young people.

Akram Azimi is a recent winner of the award, winning in 2013. He has worked with native farming communities in Australia. This is amazing because he arrived in Australia from Afghanistan when he was just 13, and English is not his first language. He excelled in school and now studies law, science, and arts in college. He felt like he needed to give something back to his adopted country, so Akram used his skills to help young people work and study in farming communities.

Marita Cheng also won the award because of her academic skills and because she helped others. She won in 2012 and was a college student at the time. Marita started Robogals Global in 2008, an organization that encourages young women to become engineers. Robogals uses fun activities to teach girls engineering and technology. Marita has worked with over 3,000 girls in Australia. The program helps girls realize that they can follow a career path in engineering.

Other winners have included famous athletes, like the swimmer Ian Thorpe (known as The Thorpedo). Like many athletes, Thorpe started very young. He started swimming at 8, and at 16, he became the youngest male world champion in history. Thorpe won the Australian of the Year award in 2000, and later that year, his amazing swimming abilities helped him break world records and win five medals – three of them gold – in the 2000 Sydney Olympics.

No matter the reasons for winning, Young Australians of the Year all have one thing in common – they had to work very hard for their success!

Culture: An article about Young Australians of the Year

1. **Look at the photos. What do you think each person did or does?**

2. **Read and listen to the article. What are some reasons that people win the Australian of the Year award?**

3. **Read the article again. Answer the questions.**
   1. How many people are chosen to compete from each state? How many people do the judges choose from?
   2. Why is Akram's work so amazing?
   3. What subject does Marita encourage girls to consider?
   4. What did Ian Thorpe achieve at 16?

4. **YOUR TURN** Work with a partner. What abilities and obligations do you think the Young Australians of the Year had? Do you have any similar abilities or obligations?

   Akram Azimi had to learn English. He...

   I had to learn English, too. I...

BE CURIOUS Find out about the Naadam Festival in Inner Mongolia. What ability are the Mongols famous for? (Workbook, p. 91)

Discovery EDUCATION
10.3 THE YOUNG AND THE BRAVE

UNIT 10 REVIEW

Vocabulary

1. **Which word or words do NOT make collocations? Sometimes, there is more than one answer.**

   1. **work:** ~~path~~   experience   ~~degree~~
   2. **application:** degree   form   fees
   3. **entrance:** exam   fees   experience
   4. **college:** course   degree   form
   5. **training:** course   path   degree

Grammar

2. **Rewrite the sentences with the words in parentheses.**

   1. Donna managed to get a job as a salesperson. (be able to)

      Donna was able to get a job as a salesperson.

   2. The athlete couldn't compete on Saturday. (not able to)

      _____

   3. The artist was able to finish the painting in 3 days. (manage to)

      _____

   4. Were you able to play the piano when you were young? (could)

      _____

   5. Walter wasn't able to pass the entrance exam. (not manage to)

      _____

3. **Write sentences and questions in the simple past or future.**

   1. the babysitter / need / pick up / the children from school / ? (past)

      Did the babysitter need to pick up the children from school?

   2. Tom / not have / take / a training course last weekend / . (past)

      _____

   3. what / application fees / I / have / pay / ? (future)

      _____

   4. Martina / not need / work / on Saturday / . (future)

      _____

   5. The chef / need / make / enough cake for 100 people / . (past)

      _____

Useful language

4. **Circle the correct answers.**

   1. **A:** I want to become a chef.

      B: I thought you wanted to be a fashion designer. ____

      a. Did you change your mind?   b. Why not?

   2. **A:** What time should we meet for dinner?

      B: ____ what time the concert starts.

      a. How about   b. That depends on

   3. **A:** Do you want to go to college or work right after you graduate?

      B: I'm not sure. ____

      a. I changed my mind.   b. I can't make up my mind.

   4. **A:** Let's get our soccer coach a thank-you gift.

      B: Good idea! ____ a colorful soccer ball?

      a. How about   b. On second thought

PROGRESS CHECK: Now I can . . .

☐ talk about my plans after graduation.
☐ discuss careers and abilities.
☐ talk about my abilities and obligations in the past.
☐ talk with someone to make decisions.
☐ write a biography about a musician.
☐ compare someone's abilities and obligations to mine.

UNITS 9–10 REVIEW, Workbook, pp. 70–71

CLIL PROJECT

10.4 LIONS IN DANGER, p. 120

Uncover Your Knowledge
UNITS 6–10 Review Game

TEAM 1
START

- Describe three things you would like to change about your room. Use passive infinitives with verbs such as *need to be* and *have to be*.
- Work with a teammate. Discuss different celebrations and describe them.
- Have a teammate tell you a story, either something he/she experienced or from a book, television show, or movie. Ask questions for more information.
- Talk about something you have/get done for you in the past, the present, and the future.
- In 15 seconds, look around the classroom and name five everyday objects.
- Role-play buying a gadget with a teammate. As the customer, ask about the price, design, features, and quality of the product. Have your teammate act as the sales clerk and answer you.
- Talk about things you enjoy doing, and say why. Use verb + gerund or infinitive.
- Look around the room. Tell a teammate about four things you see. Use modifiers to describe them. For example, *so, not really, totally, extremely, far too.*
- Have a teammate offer suggestions of things to do, such as *Let's have a party tomorrow!* Respond with an appropriate exclamation, such as *What a great idea!* See how many exclamations you can say in 30 seconds.
- Think of seven different things you do to get ready for a celebration. Name them in 20 seconds.
- Tell your teammate three things that you wish you would've done differently in your past.

INSTRUCTIONS:

- ◼ Make teams and choose game pieces.
- ◼ Put your game pieces on your team's START.
- ◼ Flip a coin to see who goes first.
- ◼ Read the first challenge. Can you do it correctly?

  Yes ➔ Continue to the next challenge.

  No ➔ Lose your turn.

The first team to do all of the challenges wins!

TEAM 2
START

- Role-play with a teammate. You are a detective and your teammate is a client who is missing something valuable from his/her home. Ask questions to try to find the missing item. Use expressions to confirm and deny what the client says.

- In 1 minute, say three sentences that each use the same word with and without *un-*.

- Tell a teammate a story that takes place over time. It can be a story you know, a historical situation, or something that happened to you. Be sure to use time clauses: *before, after, when,* and any others.

- In 15 seconds, say five collocations for training and qualifications, such as *college degree*.

- Talk about taking a trip. Use these verbs in *-ing* form as subjects: *travel, watch, have, see*. For example, *Seeing the pyramids in Egypt is a dream of mine.*

- Imagine that you and your teammate are given a million dollars, but you can only give it to charities and volunteer organizations. How do you donate the money? Decide how to spend or split the money between organizations. Explain your reasons.

- Talk with a teammate about mysteries from the past. Use past modals of speculation.

- Use reporting verbs to talk about your favorite scene from a movie or TV show.

- Tell your teammate four different things you heard people say yesterday. Say two of them as reported speech, one as quoted speech, and one that uses the *-ing* form.

- Play charades. Act out a job and have your teammates guess what it is. See how many you can complete in 1 minute.

- Imagine you are a teacher. Tell a teammate about things you'll make your students do and those you'll let them do.

- Explain to a teammate at least six different elements of a story. Give a definition for each.

■ GRAMMAR

■ VOCABULARY

■ USEFUL LANGUAGE

This page intentionally left blank.

Passive infinitive, p. 57

The passive is the main verb + to be + a past participle. The main verb usually expresses thinking or speaking, for example: be, have, know, want, need, expect, like, believe, and ask.

Present	Past
The bottle **needs to be closed** with a black top. Moser **likes to be challenged**.	The lamp **didn't have to be plugged** in. He **didn't expect to be known** around the world for his invention.

1. Complete the sentences with passive infinitives. Use the forms in parentheses.

   1. Kyle _____ from his classes on Tuesday. (ask / excuse, *simple past*)

   2. We _____ with the workshop by 5:00 p.m. (expect / do, *simple past*)

   3. Ms. Anderson _____ the same questions twice. (not like / ask, *simple present*)

   4. My computer _____ at the end of the day. (need / shut down, *simple present*)

   5. Jeremy _____ for his invention. (want / remember, *simple present*)

Review of causative *have/get*, p. 59

Use causative have/get *in situations where someone else does something for you or when it's not important who is doing the action. You can use* have *or* get. *They have similar meanings.*
Use have/get *+ an object + past participle with the present, past, and future.*

	Active	Passive/Causative
Simple present	Someone **cleans** her house on Thursdays.	She **has** her house **cleaned** on Thursdays.
Simple past	Someone **delivered** the lamp today.	We **got** the lamp **delivered** today.
Present continuous	No one **is sending** the lamp to the man's house.	The man **isn't having** a lamp **sent** to his house.
Past continuous	Someone **was printing** the inventor's paper.	The inventor **was getting** his paper **printed** in New York City.
Future with *will*	I **will ask** someone **to make** a designer battery charger for my sister.	I **will get** a designer battery charger **made** for my sister.
Modals	**Should** I **ask** someone to **wrap** them for you?	Should I **have** them **wrapped** for you?

2. Complete the sentences with causative *have* or *get*. Use the verbs and tense in parentheses.

   1. Marcos _____ his tablet _____. (have / repair / *simple past*)

   2. Mia and Lou _____ their car _____ once a month. (get / clean / *simple present*)

   3. I _____ my website _____ this week. (have / update / *present continuous*)

   4. We _____ our phones _____ at the store in the mall. (have / upgrade / *modal: could*)

   5. _____ you _____ your clothes _____ at Sam's Laundry Service? (get / wash / *past continuous*)

   6. Jeanne _____ her kitchen cabinets _____ by a professional. (get / make / *future with* will)

Verb + -ing form (gerund) or infinitive, p. 67

Many verbs are followed by the -ing form of a verb or an infinitive. Some verbs can be followed by either an -ing form or an infinitive with no change in meaning. Others can be followed by either an -ing form or an infinitive, but the meaning changes.

Verb + -ing form: consider discuss enjoy finish keep miss	**Consider having** a theme party. Some people **don't enjoy hosting** them.
Verb + infinitive: decide learn expect need plan want	Decide what food you **want to make**. Do you **need to have** the party at a bigger place?
Verb + -ing form or infinitive: begin hate like love prefer start	Everybody **loves going** to parties! Everybody **loves to go** to parties!
Verb + -ing form or infinitive with change in meaning: forget remember try	Don't **forget to plan** a budget. (= not forget to do something) I'll never **forget going** to my first birthday party. (= not forgetting that something happened) I **tried to work** as a party planner, but I couldn't find a job. (= try something, but not succeed at it) I **tried working** as a party planner, but I didn't like the job. (= try something to see if it works)

1. **Write a check (✓) for the correct sentences. Correct the mistakes in the incorrect sentences.**
    1. ☐ We discussed to have the holiday party at my house.
    2. ☐ I hate going to parties by myself.
    3. ☐ Alex kept putting up decorations even after we finished.
    4. ☐ We planned playing rock music at the party for several hours.
    5. ☐ Lori remembered to prepare special foods with her grandmother when she was young.
    6. ☐ We decided watching the parade on Clinton Street.

-ing form (gerund) as subject; by/for + -ing form, p. 69

You can use the -ing form as the subject of a sentence. When it's the subject, the verb is singular.

Traveling to Italy is always great.
Watching the monkeys is very entertaining.
Not going to the festival would be a mistake.

The -ing form can also be used after by to show how to do something and after for to show the purpose or use of something.

Let's start **by returning** to Harbin.
The weather is perfect **for making** ice statues.

2. **Complete the sentences with the -ing form of the verbs. Add *by* or *for* when needed.**
    1. I think _____ (go) to festivals is fun only if they aren't crowded.
    2. I like to celebrate my birthday _____ (have) a small party with friends.
    3. _____ (watch) movies at a film festival is exciting.
    4. I told my friends that _____ (no remember) my birthday is a bad idea!
    5. A park is a good place _____ (get) together with friends.

Time clauses; present participle clauses, p. 77

Use time clauses to show the order of events in the past, present, and future.
Use before to show that the event in the time clause happened second.

The Atlantic Avenue Tunnel was made in 1844 **before** the subway system was created.
  FIRST EVENT   SECOND EVENT

Use after to show the event in the time clause happened first.

After the news spreads, Bob becomes a local hero.
  FIRST EVENT   SECOND EVENT

Use when to show that both events happened at the same time.

They will search for a steam train in the tunnel **when** they have enough money.

You can use the -ing form (gerund) of a verb after before and after.

Before searching for the tunnel, Bob heard about it on a radio program.
Bob finds an old map **after searching** city records for eight months.

1. Circle the correct answers.

   1. The divers took a photo of the unusual fish **before** / **when** they saw it.
   2. We bought tickets to the concert after **heard** / **hearing** the band's music.
   3. The detective will take a vacation after he **catches** / **will catch** the criminal.
   4. **When** / **After** we go to the museum, we'll go home.

Reported speech, p. 79

Use reported speech and reported questions to tell others what another person said. In both reported speech and reported questions, the verbs usually change tenses.

Quoted speech	Reported speech
She said, "I **am leaving** the dolls."	She admitted that she **was leaving** the dolls.
She said, "I **was watching** TV."	She wrote that she **had been watching** TV.
He asked, "**When will** you **be talking** to her?"	He asked me **when** I **would be talking** to her.
He asked, "Are you keeping her secret?"	He asked me **if I was keeping** her secret.

Infinitives can be used with these reporting verbs: agree, claim, decide.

I **agreed to keep** it a secret.	She **claimed to know** who had done it.

The -ing form can be used with these reporting verbs: recommend, insist on, admit to.

She **insisted on keeping** the doll.	I **recommend posting** a question online.

Imperative clauses

Change an imperative to a reported imperative using infinitive verbs.

Quoted imperative	Reported imperative
He said, "**Tell** me about it!"	He told her **to tell** him about it.
She said, "**Don't tell** anyone."	She said **not to tell** anyone.

2. Put the words in the correct order to make sentences.

   1. said / in the ocean / not to / swim / my parents

   _____

   2. recommended / a mystery novel / reading / Paisley

   _____

   3. to find / I / I / was / said / trying / the answer / that

   _____

   4. been / watching / if I / the news / had / Doug / asked me

   _____

Unit 8 | 113

Third conditional, p. 87

> Use the third conditional sentences to describe imaginary situations and impossible consequences. Use if + past perfect for the imaginary and untrue situation in the past. Use would (not) + have + past participle for the impossible consequence.
>
> If he **hadn't heard** those noises, he **wouldn't have gone** on an adventure.
> If the teenager **had stolen** Gracie, he **would have gotten** away.
>
> What **would have happened if** the thief **had stolen** Gracie?
> He **would have gotten** away.
>
> **Would** the chicken **have become** a hero **if** it **hadn't saved** Lucky?
> Yes, it **would have**. / No, it **wouldn't have**.

1. **Write sentences and questions with the third conditional.**

   1. if / Ted / not read / that story / he / not be / scared /.
      If Ted hadn't read that story, he wouldn't have been scared.

   2. Cynthia / take photos of the hoodoos / if her camera / work /.
      _____

   3. what / you / do / if / someone / steal / your wallet /?
      _____

   4. you / call / the police / if / you / see / strange lights last night /?
      _____

   5. if / we / walk / a few more miles / we / reach / the top of the mountain /.
      _____

Past modals of speculation, p. 89

> Use past modals of speculation to show how certain you are about a past event. Form past modals with modal + have + past participle.

Affirmative	Negative
Not sure: Hoodoos **may have been** people. You **might have seen** more hoodoos. Rivers **could have formed** them.	**Not sure:** They **may not have been** nice people. He **might not have liked** them.
Sure: The Legend People **must have made** Coyote mad.	**Sure:** People **couldn't have made** them. The Legend People **must not have known** that it was a trick.

2. **Complete the sentences with a modal + *have* + past particle of the verbs in parentheses. ✓ = sure. ✗ = not sure. Sometimes more than one answer is possible.**

   1. Kyle _____ (not see, ✓) that movie. He doesn't like science fiction movies.

   2. Leslie _____ (not take, ✗) that photo of the cliff dwellings. She's never been to Mesa Verde.

   3. Claudia and Leo _____ (walk, ✓) to work. Their car is at the mechanic's shop.

   4. Sarah _____ (not like, ✗) my story. She didn't say much about it.

   5. The movie _____ (take, ✗) place in Japan. Some of the city scenes looked like they were in Tokyo.

   6. You _____ (not get, ✓) much sleep last night. You sent me an email at 2:00 a.m.!

Past ability, p. 97

Use could, was/were able to, *and* managed to *to talk about past abilities.*
Use could *for both general and specific abilities.*

GENERAL:	SPECIFIC:
What **could** you **do**?	**Could** she **drive** when she was 15?
I **couldn't do** anything.	Yes, she **could**. She **could drive** well.
I **could learn** to do anything!	No, she **couldn't**. She **couldn't drive** yet.

Use was/were able to *and* managed to *for specific abilities only.*

How **was** she **able to learn** so much?	How **did** she **manage to pay** for it?
She **was able to watch** videos online.	She **managed to save** money.
She **wasn't able to take** a course.	She **didn't manage to get** a free car.
Were they **able to fix** the car?	**Did** you **manage to fix** the car?
Yes, they **were**. / No, they **weren't**.	Yes, I **did**. / No, I **didn't**.

1. **Complete the sentences with *could (not), (not) be able to*, and *(not) managed to* and the verb in parentheses. Sometimes more than one answer is possible.**

   1. Unfortunately, Jeff _____ (gain) much work experience before he started his job.
   2. I _____ (work) last year because I wasn't old enough to have a job.
   3. We _____ (pay) the application fees for our photography class on Friday morning because our parents gave us the money.
   4. _____ (you / get) to your training course at 6:00 p.m.?

Modal expressions for past and future, p. 99

Use (not) had to *and* (not) need to *for obligations and necessities in the past.*

What **did** you **need to learn** about?	What **did** he **have to do**?
I **needed to learn** about fashion.	He **had to take** a training course.
I **didn't need to learn** about chemistry.	He **didn't have to get** a college degree.
Did he **need to take** training courses?	**Did** they **need to work** on weekends?
Yes, he **did**.	Yes, they **did**.
No, he **didn't**.	No, they **didn't**.

Use will (not) have to *and* will (not) need to *for obligations and necessities in the future.*

What courses **will** you **have to take**?	When **will** she **need to finish** the design?
I **will have to take** more training courses.	She **will need to finish** by Friday.
I **won't have to take** any college courses.	She **won't need to finish** by tomorrow.
Will he **have to take** more courses?	**Will** they **need to pay** an entrance fee?
Yes, he **will**.	Yes, they **will**.
No, he **won't**.	No, they **won't**.

2. **Put the words in the correct order to make sentences and questions.**

   1. finish / my degree / I / to / have /next year / will /.
      _____
   2. needed / her application / Shelly / to / last month / fee / pay /.
      _____
   3. you / need / get / will / a babysitter / tomorrow night / to /?
      _____
   4. need / an entrance / pay / Mariah / fee / didn't / for the art class / to /.
      _____
   5. to / exam / have / entrance / take / when / the / Greg / will /?
      _____

CLIL PROJECT

Making MUSIC

1. Read these descriptions of the parts of an acoustic guitar. Then label the diagram below.

Body:	The main part of the guitar
Bridge:	The lower parts of the strings are attached to this
Frets:	You press the strings down on these to make sound
Head:	The upper part of the guitar
Soundhole:	A round hole in the body that lets the sound out
Strings:	You pick these to make sound
Tuning keys/pegs:	You turn these to change the pitch of the strings

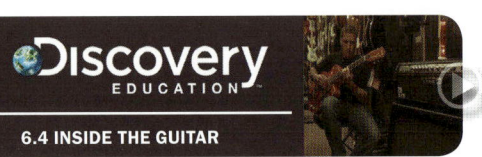

Discovery EDUCATION
6.4 INSIDE THE GUITAR

2. Watch the video. Number the stages of making a guitar 1–5.

_____ They spray colors onto the guitar.

_____ They add the strings.

_____ They add the frets by hand.

_____ They use big machines to make the bodies.

_____ They put small magnets under the strings.

3. Complete the sentences with the correct words.

| acoustic | amplifies | original | revolution | solid | waves |

1. Traditional guitars are also known as _____ guitars.
2. The body of a traditional guitar _____ the sound.
3. Electric guitars have a _____ body.
4. We see guitars that look like an _____ Gibson guitar of 1952.
5. When the strings move over the magnets they create _____.
6. The electric guitar was part of a _____ in music.

PROJECT

What's your favorite musical instrument – the piano, violin, trumpet, drums, or something else? Make a poster advertising music lessons for this instrument. Say why other students should want to learn this instrument.

Music Lessons

- What types of music can you play?
- Can you make money playing this instrument?
- What is the history of the instrument?
- Have any famous people played this instrument?
- In which parts of the world is this instrument popular?

118 | CLIL Project | Unit 6

Bringing HISTORY TO LIFE

The American Revolutionary War

By the 1760s, conflict was beginning between the British government in London and the 13 British colonies on the eastern side of North America. The colonists resisted the British government's control, sometimes violently, and a full war began in 1775. The colonies signed the Declaration of Independence, declaring themselves free of British rule. Six years later, the British army surrendered at Yorktown. George Washington, who led the American army, became the new country's first president in 1789.

The American Civil War

In the middle of the next century, the northern states were more industrial, while the southern states had large plantations that grew cotton and tobacco and were worked by slaves. In 1860, Abraham Lincoln, who was opposed to slavery, was elected president. Eleven southern states broke away from the rest of the country, and a war started in 1861. Despite early victories, the South surrendered four years later. Throughout the war, over a million people lost their lives, including President Lincoln, who was assassinated just days after it ended. In 1865, slavery became illegal in the United States.

1. **Decide if these sentences describe the Revolutionary War (*RW*) or the Civil War (*CW*).**
   1. Eleven states left the United States. ____
   2. The American colonies fought for independence. ____
   3. One side was more successful at the start, but ended up losing. ____
   4. British soldiers were involved in this war. ____
   5. The president did not live long after the end of this war. ____

2. **Watch the video. Number these events 1–5 in the order that they happened.**
   ____ The American Civil War began.
   ____ Reenactors re-create previous battles.
   ____ There was a war between Britain and the American colonies.
   ____ President Lincoln made a speech at Gettysburg.
   ____ The American colonies declared their independence from Britain.

Discovery EDUCATION
8.4 RELIVING HISTORY

PROJECT What events in the history of your country do you think should be reenacted? Imagine you are organizing a reenactment event. Write a list of instructions for the reenactors:
- What they need to wear
- What they should bring with them for the reenactment
- What they should bring to eat
- Where and when they should arrive
- What will happen during the day

CLIL PROJECT

Saving the LIONS

1. **This map of Kenya shows where the people live and where the national parks are. Kenya's population is increasing at 2.7 percent per year, but the wildlife is decreasing. Discuss these questions:**
   - How will Kenya's economy be different if its wildlife disappears?
   - Why do people sometimes destroy wildlife?
   - How can local people protect the wildlife?

10.4 LIONS IN DANGER

2. **Watch the video. Complete the sentences with the correct numbers.**

   | ¼ | 20 | 20–30 | 35 | 25,000 |

   1. Only _____ lions live in Africa today.
   2. Jeff Corwin has worked with wildlife for almost _____ years.
   3. More than _____ million people live in Kenya.
   4. More than _____ of a million people live outside the national park.
   5. In this region, people used to kill _____ lions a year.

3. **Circle the correct answers.**

   1. The number of lions in Africa is falling because of _____.
      a. people   b. climate   c. both a & b
   2. In the last hundred years, the human population around the park has _____.
      a. increased   b. decreased   c. not changed much
   3. People used to kill lions mainly _____.
      a. to protect their animals   b. to protect themselves   c. to sell their skins
   4. They don't kill lions now because of _____.
      a. education   b. money/compensation   c. both a & b

PROJECT Think of a species in danger, in your own country or somewhere else. What is being done to protect these animals? Research the animal and write a fact sheet about its characteristics and its chances of survival. Then look at all the fact sheets from your class. With the other students, work out a plan to protect a species in danger.

Uncover 4 Combo B
Lynne Robertson

Workbook

CAMBRIDGE UNIVERSITY PRESS

Discovery EDUCATION

6 It's the Little Things.

VOCABULARY Everyday objects

1 **Match the sentences with the pictures.**

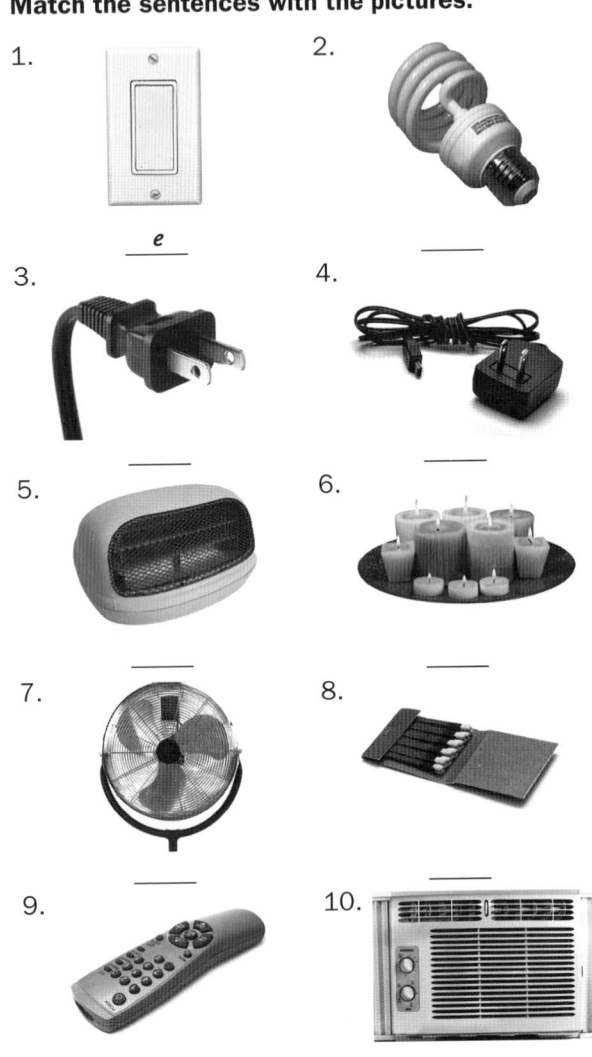

1. _____
2. _____
3. _____
4. _____
5. _____
6. _____
7. _____
8. _____
9. _____
10. _____

(Picture 1: e)

a. I can't find the remote control for the television!
b. Don't forget to put out the candles.
c. Do you have a spare phone charger?
d. It's hot in here! Turn on the fan, please.
e. Can you turn on the light? The switch is over there.
f. I'm a bit chilly. Let's turn off the air conditioner.
g. Have you seen the matches?
h. When I traveled to London, I couldn't use my hairdryer! The plug was different!
i. Don't forget to turn off that heater before you go to bed.
j. The stores only sell those new light bulbs that save energy.

2 **Read the situations and circle the correct answers.**

1. Jan is driving in her car. It is cold. What should she turn on?
   a. the charger   b. the fan   c. (the heater)

2. The power goes out in Ha Jin's apartment at night. What can he use for light?
   a. a candle   b. a light bulb   c. a switch

3. Tracy is camping. She has gathered logs. What does she need to start a fire?
   a. a fan   b. matches   c. a remote control

4. Now the power is on in Ha Jin's apartment. What does he need to press to turn on the light?
   a. a heater   b. a plug   c. a switch

5. Now the lamp in Ha Jin's apartment doesn't work. What does he need to replace?
   a. the air conditioner   b. the light bulb   c. the remote control

6. Jan is driving in her car, and now it is very hot. What should she turn on?
   a. the air conditioner   b. the light bulb   c. matches

7. Tracy's cell phone won't turn on. What does she probably need to make it work?
   a. a charger   b. a heater   c. a switch

8. At night, the air is very still and it is hot in Jan's hotel room. What does she turn on?
   a. a candle   b. a fan   c. a heater

9. The switch for the fan in Jan's hotel room doesn't work. What should she check?
   a. the charger   b. the light bulb   c. the plug

10. Tracy wants to watch a movie. What does she use to turn on the TV?
    a. an air condiioner   b. a plug   c. a remote control

3 Answer the questions with the words from Exercise 1 and your own information.

1. When does your family use candles?
   We use candles for birthdays and special
   dinners.
   _____

2. Which months of the year do you use a heater?
   _____
   _____

3. Which months of the year do you use a fan or an air conditioner?
   _____
   _____

4. Which two items from Exercise 1 do you use the most? For what?
   _____
   _____

GRAMMAR Passive infinitive

1 Complete the chart using the passive infinitive.

	Present	Past
1. want/know	Raul _wants to be known_ for his popularity.	Raul _wanted to be known_ for his singing ability.
2. have/charge	Lara's phone _____ every few hours.	Lara's phone _____ overnight.
3. like/laugh at	The comedian _____ when he's funny.	The comedian _didn't_ _____ when he made the mistake.
4. expect/treat	We _____ fairly in school.	We _____ fairly at summer camp.
5. not have/pay	The full price _____ by students.	The full price _____ when the students went to the theater.
6. not need/see	This movie _____ by anyone over the age of five.	This movie _____ in 3-D.

2 Complete the paragraph with the present and past passive infinitive forms of the verbs.

Our new apartment in Miami was a mess when we moved in! We ¹_didn't expect it to be messed up_ (not expect it / mess up) because it was clean when we first saw it.

The air conditioner was really dusty. It ² _____ (need / clean) right away because it was hot when we moved in. It works now, which is good. The plugs on one wall didn't work either. We had to put the sofa and table, things that ³ _____ (not have / plug in), against that wall. They still need to be fixed. And all of the light bulbs ⁴ _____ (have / replace) as soon as we find the time to do it.

At least the carpet ⁵ _____ (not have / clean) when we moved in. The heater is broken, but it ⁶ _____ (not need / fix) right away. It's so hot here right now, we don't expect to use it for months!

Passive with modals

3 Rewrite the present sentences from Exercise 1 as modals. Use _must, should, might,_ or _had better._ More than one answer may be possible.

1. Raul _wants to be_ known for his popularity. >
   Raul must be known for his popularity.
2. _____
3. _____
4. _____
5. _____
6. _____

4 Complete the sentences using your own ideas. Use the passive infinitive or modals.

1. My smartphone needs _to be turned off at school_.
   My smartphone needs _____.
2. His new laptop might _____.
3. The candle has _____.
4. The matches must _____.
5. We didn't expect _____.

VOCABULARY Modifiers

1 Circle seven more modifiers. Then write them in the chart.

so / not really / extremely / far too / totally / ridiculously / kind of / a little bit

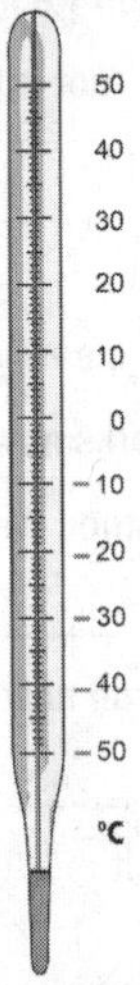

1. _ _ _ _ _ _ _ _ _ _ _ _
2. _ _ _ _ _ _ _ _
3. _ _ _ _ _ _ _
4. s o
5. _ _ _ _ _ _ _
6. _ _ _ _ _ _
7. _ _ _ _ _ _ _ _ _ _
8. _ _ _ _ _ _ _ _ _

2 Look at the pictures. Circle the correct answers.

1. My bike is **not really / ridiculously** small. I don't think I can ride it anymore.

2. Let's turn off the air conditioner. It's **a little bit / far too** chilly in here! My hands are freezing!

3. I want a new laptop, but this one's **not really / so** expensive. I don't have enough money to buy it.

4. That dress is **kind of / far too** nice to wear while you paint your room!

5. That watch is **kind of / not really** cool. But I don't think it has enough features.

6. My grandmother thinks it's **extremely / not really** important to have a smartphone. She still doesn't have one.

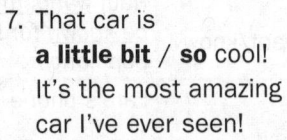

7. That car is **a little bit / so** cool! It's the most amazing car I've ever seen!

8. Personally, I'm **not really / totally** bored with that social networking site. I'm going to quit visiting it.

3 Complete the sentences with a word or phrase from each box and your own ideas.

extremely	colorful
far too	cool
a little bit	dangerous
kind of	difficult
not really	easy
ridiculously	expensive
so	old
totally	small

1. *My brother's smartphone is far too old to take videos.*
2. _____
3. _____
4. _____
5. _____
6. _____
7. _____
8. _____

GRAMMAR Review of causative have/get

1 Match the active sentences with the passive/causative sentences.

Active	Passive/Causative
1. Someone repairs her bike after a race. **b**	a. She isn't having her bike repaired after the race.
2. Someone repaired her bike after the race. ___	b. She has her bike repaired after a race.
3. No one is repairing her bike after the race. ___	c. She'll get her bike repaired after the race.
4. She'll ask someone to repair her bike after the race. ___	d. Must she have her bike repaired after the race?
5. Must she get someone to repair her bike after the race? ___	e. She got her bike repaired after the race.

2 Put the words in the correct order to make sentences.

1. his charger / got / fixed / last night / Andrew / .
   Andrew got his charger fixed last night.
2. to do / for me / get / I / can never / my brother / my homework / .
   _____
3. I / cut / the / have / lawn / Should / you / for / ?
   _____
4. camera / isn't / his / boy / The / checked / getting / today / .
   _____
5. weekend / get / school / painted / The / won't / this / .
   _____
6. cleaned / on / have / team uniforms / We / our / weekends / .
   _____

3 Rewrite the sentences. Use the tense and voice (active or causative) in parentheses.

1. Someone <u>paints</u> Mike's skateboard on Friday. (simple past/active)
   Someone *painted Mike's skateboard on Friday.*
2. I <u>will fix</u> my laptop this weekend. (future with will/causative)
   I will _____
3. Someone <u>cuts</u> Tom's hair every three months. (simple present/passive)
   Tom _____
4. The man <u>isn't having anyone set up</u> his website. (present continuous/active) No one _____ the man's website.
5. Someone professionally <u>photographed</u> Elizabeth's birthday party. (simple past/causative)
   Elizabeth _____

CONVERSATION: Buying a gadget

1 Put the words in the correct order to complete the phrase. Match the phrases to the second part of questions 1–6.

> ~~you / could / show /~~
> it / does / have /
> model / is / which /
> it / to / is / easy / use /
> is / how / good / it /
> does / how / it / long /

1. *Could you show* us how to use the video function?
2. _____ last before you have to charge it?
3. _____ the newest?
4. _____ compared to the previous version?
5. _____ or do I need to read the instructions?
6. _____ any extra batteries?

2 Complete the conversation with the phrases from Exercise 1.

Hiroki: Excuse me. ¹ *Could you show* me this digital camera?

Salesperson: Here you are.

Hiroki: Thank you.

Emma: Hiroki, that one's OK. But ² _____ to use in the water? I don't think that kind is waterproof.

Hiroki: Oh, you're right. But ³ _____?

Emma: Yeah, it's really easy because it's totally basic. But look, it says it's not waterproof.

Emma (to salesperson): Excuse me, ⁴ _____ the waterproof one?

Salesperson: This one is.

Emma: ⁵ _____ take to charge?

Salesperson: About two hours.

Emma: See, Hiroki? That's pretty fast.

Hiroki: ⁶ _____ GPS?

Salesperson: Of course, it does.

Emma: Oh, gosh. Look at the price!

Hiroki: Wow, that's expensive!

READING TO WRITE

1 Combine the underlined sentences with *while* or *whereas*. Make any other changes necessary.

Bass Boss Headphones v2
posted by Josephine

This review is for Bass Boss Headphones v2. I found them on sale online for $89.99. ¹That seems ridiculously expensive for a pair of headphones. It's about ten dollars less than the older version and about ten times better!

First of all, the new v2 model headphones sound *amazing*. ²The v1 headphones sound good. These sound great. Your ears will enjoy cleaner high notes, deeper bass notes, and an overall crisp sound. And they have excellent sound-elimination technology!

³I liked using the old headphones on my way to school. I love the new ones even more. I can hear every note even when I'm on a noisy bus! They're also useful for studying languages. I plug mine in to my laptop when I study English.

⁴The v1 had a good design. These fit better. ⁵The v2 model looks sleeker. The previous version was kind of clunky. ⁶The v1 model only came in black or white. This new model comes in 20 fun colors, like orange or green. The new version is lighter, too!

Finally, there's a new feature for v2. You can press a button on the cord to mute the sound so you can hear what's going on around you. Perfect for when your mom's calling you to come to dinner.

I think these are great headphones. They have more useful features than the previous version. I recommend buying them on sale.

1. _While that seems ridiculously expensive for a pair of headphones, it's ten dollars less than the older version and about ten times better!_
2. _____
3. _____
4. _____
5. _____
6. _____

2 Read the article in Exercise 1 again. Circle the correct answers.

1. What does Josephine say about the price of the Bass Boss Headphones v2?
   a. She says it was ten dollars.
   b. She says they weren't on sale.
   c. (She says they cost a lot.)

2. What is different about the v2 model headphones?
   a. They're lighter, and they sound better, fit better, and come in more colors.
   b. They're ridiculously expensive, kind of clunky, and noisy.
   c. They only come in orange or green.

3. What are they useful for?
   a. for recording sounds
   b. for listening to music and studying
   c. for hearing your mother call you

4. What new feature does the v2 model have?
   a. It can be plugged into a laptop.
   b. It can be found on sale.
   c. The sound can be muted.

5. What is her recommendation?
   a. not to buy it
   b. to buy it on sale
   c. to buy the v1 headphones

REVIEW UNITS 5-6

1 Circle the correct answers.

1. This plug looks **a little bit** / **ridiculously** bent. I think it needs to be replaced.
2. I **dislike** / **feel** the position of this switch. It's difficult to reach.
3. This remote control is **absolutely** / **hardly** amazing! It can turn on **fairly** / **nearly** everything in this room!
4. Can we turn off the air conditioner now? I **appreciate** / **think** the room is cool enough.
5. I **recommend** / **respect** these light bulbs for your art studio. They are nice and bright.
6. I **admire** / **recommend** that you get a new phone charger. This one works **not really** / **so** slowly!
7. I **hate** / **respect** this fan. It's **far too** / **not really** noisy!
8. I'm **pretty** / **ridiculously** satisfied with this heater. It works **hardly** / **perfectly** fine, even though it was inexpensive.

2 Match the sentences from Exercise 1 with the pictures.

a. _1_    b. ____
c.  ____ d. ____ 
e.  ____ f. ____ 
g.  ____ h. ____ 

3 Cross out the word that doesn't belong in each category.

1. Expressing an opinion:
   feel   hate   respect   ridiculously
2. Everyday objects:
   a little bit   a fan   a plug   a switch
3. Words that modify others:
   extremely   far too   kind of   remote control
4. Adverbs that show degree:
   hardly   nearly   pricey   pretty

4 Put the words in the correct order to make sentences.

1. my grandfather / I / cleaned / the yard / for / get / will / .
   I will get the yard cleaned for my grandfather.
2. it / fixed / for / have / I / you / Should / ?
   _____
3. the car / cleaned / got / Friday / on / They / .
   _____
4. of / blog posts / get / people / Her / read / by / a lot / .
   _____
5. delivered / aren't / a pizza / Our friends / house / to / their / having / .
   _____
6. her / Kim / mother's / have / replaced / air conditioner / will / .
   _____

5 Rewrite the sentences. Change the verbs from active to passive.

1. People know Maya for her beautiful voice.
   Maya is known for her beautiful voice.

2. Nobody needed to turn the air conditioner on.
   _____

3. Someone put out the candles before bedtime.
   _____

4. People know Terry for his inventions, and he likes that.
   _____

5. We turned our phones off during class, which Mrs. Cook expected.
   _____

6 Complete the conversations with tag questions.

1. **A:** You still listen to Katy Perry, _don't you_?
   B: Not as much as I used to.

2. **A:** You've already seen *Guardians of the Galaxy*, _____?
   B: A long time ago.

3. **A:** You're buying the latest smartphone, _____?
   B: Not right away.

4. **A:** That was an exciting game last night, _____?
   B: I'll say! I was on the edge of my seat!

5. **A:** Sports stars should make less money, _____?
   B: I guess so. But the really good ones sell a lot of tickets.

6. **A:** Rap music is getting kind of old, _____?
   B: Kind of. I like it, but I just don't listen to it as much as I used to.

7 Combine the sentences using defining or non-defining relative clauses. More than one answer may be correct.

1. I think people are desperate for attention. They go on reality TV shows.
   I think people who are desperate for attention go on reality TV shows.

2. My friend Rebecca was on a reality TV show. She's an interior designer.
   _____
   _____

3. Rebecca was starting a design business. Starting a design business is hard to do.
   _____
   _____

4. She got on a reality show. The reality show redecorates people's homes.
   _____
   _____

5. They redecorated for people. The people's homes had been ruined in a flood.
   _____
   _____

8 Complete the conversation.

~~Could you show me~~	It seems to me that
Does it have	That's a good point.
How good is	Which model

Sophia: Hey, Noah. ¹ _Could you show me_ your tablet?

Noah: Sure. Are you thinking about buying one?

Sophia: Yeah. ² _____ a video camera?

Noah: Yes, it does.

Sophia: ³ _____ the video quality, though? I need to use it for my video class assignments.

Noah: It's pretty good.

Sophia: ⁴ _____ has the best quality camera?

Noah: Oh, not this one. ⁵ _____ you'd be happier with the upgraded version. But it's more expensive.

Julia: Yeah, but if I can take better videos, that will help me get a better grade in class, right?

Noah: Oh, well, yeah. ⁶ _____

7 Have a Ball!

VOCABULARY Celebration phrases

1 Unscramble the words to make celebration phrases. Then number the pictures.

1. A L P Y C S U M I — *play music*
2. S R E S D   P U — _____
3. T U P   P U   R E D O O N S I A C T — _____
4. C H A W T   A   A D E R P A — _____
5. E V H A   A   D O O G   M I T E — _____

6. V E G I   A   T R E E N P S — _____
7. E S T   F O F   R O R K I W E S F — _____
8. P E A R R E P   L I S P A C E   O D O F — _____
9. D L H O   A   S T O N E C T — _____

2 Circle the correct answers.

1. Our neighbor **has a good time / puts up decorations** for nearly every holiday. People from all over town drive by his house to see them.
2. My favorite part of celebrating is when people **give a present / set off fireworks**. They look so pretty in the night sky.
3. My grandfather won't go with us anymore to **prepare special foods / watch the parade.** He said he doesn't like crowds.
4. Tino comes to every party. He really likes to **have a good time / hold a contest**.
5. Bridget likes to **dress up / play music** at parties, but she'll let you suggest songs.

6. I love costume parties! Especially when they **hold a contest / prepare special food**. I usually have creative ideas and win.
7. My boyfriend doesn't like going to weddings because he doesn't like to **dress up / watch a parade**.
8. My family always **plays music / prepares special food** for our celebrations. We've been making the same delicious dishes for years!
9. My brother likes to **give presents / hold contests**. He makes all his gifts by hand.

44 | Unit 7

GRAMMAR Verb + -ing form (gerund) or infinitive

1 Circle the correct answers. If both answers are possible, circle both.

1. Tiffany hates **going / to go** to parties.
2. Michael learned **dancing / to dance** for his wedding.
3. They're considering **having / to have** a New Year's party.
4. We haven't forgotten **bringing / to bring** a dish to the party.
5. My uncle started **grilling / to grill** the chicken already.
6. My younger sister tried **staying up / to stay up** until midnight on New Year's Eve, but she fell asleep at 11 o'clock.

2 Correct the sentences with either the infinitive or -ing form. If the sentences are already correct, write *correct*.

1. What kind of music do you want ~~playing~~ *to play* at the party? _____
2. Do you remember to go a concert for the first time? _____
3. Some people don't like to dress up in costumes. _____
4. My sister doesn't enjoy to eat cake on her birthday. _____
5. My cousin plans having her graduation party at home. _____
6. Don't forget cleaning the house before the party. _____
7. Rachel and Tom discussed to have their wedding in Sonoma. _____
8. Heather loves to sing karaoke at parties. _____

3 Put the words in the correct order to make sentences. When necessary, change the verbs to the infinitive or the -ing form. More than one answer may be possible.

1. I / can't / a / was / remember / when / have / two / birthday party / I / .

   I can't remember having a birthday party when I was two.

2. Tracy / arrive / at / on time / our house / expects / .

   _____

3. try / the / eat / once / at / all / Don't / candy / .

   _____

4. The / the / start / teacher / game / party / prefers / with / a / .

   _____

5. Elliot / have / his / clowns / birthday / doesn't / party / at / enjoy / .

   _____

6. celebration / get / The / noisy / after / began / the / first fireworks / .

   _____

4 Write sentences that are true for you. Use the phrases *(not) enjoy, (not) want, love, hate,* and *(not) forget* with the infinitive or the -ing forms of the verbs.

1. ride a bike

   I love riding a bike.

2. dress up

   _____

3. give a present

   _____

4. prepare special food

   _____

5. put up decorations

   _____

6. set off fireworks

   _____

VOCABULARY Descriptive adjectives

1 Circle nine more adjectives.

A	I	M	P	R	E	S	S	I	V	E	L
N	W	S	K	R	T	S	C	A	R	Y	I
I	E	T	S	Q	I	N	O	I	S	Y	V
A	Q	M	E	S	S	Y	V	H	R	E	E
T	R	A	D	I	T	I	O	N	A	L	L
H	Z	S	T	U	N	N	I	N	G	W	Y
P	E	A	C	E	F	U	L	V	W	A	N
L	A	V	P	J	P	Y	H	N	I	C	Q
A	W	M	G	C	R	O	W	D	E	D	H
S	Q	N	P	O	Q	H	T	K	O	E	S
E	Y	X	J	R	F	S	M	Z	C	J	Y
J	X	J	D	C	O	L	O	R	F	U	L

2 Circle the correct answers.

1. Yumi told me about the Japanese festival of *hanami*, or flower viewing. People have a picnic under the cherry blossoms in the spring. She said the women often wear a *kimono* during the *hanami* festival. A *kimono* is a kind of **crowded / lively / traditional** Japanese robe. *Hanami* sounded like a lovely, **crowded / noisy / peaceful** nature festival. But Yumi told me it was very **lively / stunning / traditional**, with lots of people singing and dancing.

2. On New Year's Eve, everyone in our city gathers downtown to wait for midnight. There are so many people! It's very **colorful / crowded / traditional**, but it feels safe and fun. When the clock strikes midnight, everyone cheers and it gets quite **colorful / messy / noisy**. My favorite part of New Year's is when the city sets off the fireworks. This year's fireworks display was particularly **peaceful / crowded / stunning**! I loved it. My younger brother didn't like the fireworks, though. He thought they were loud and **impressive / peaceful / scary**.

3. Ed went to a festival in India where people throw bright powder on each other. His photos are amazing. He has some beautiful shots of colored powder flying through the air. The powder is so **colorful / peaceful / traditional**. And it's **colorful / impressive / peaceful** that he didn't get powder all over his camera! He said the festival was wonderful, but it was very **crowded / messy / noisy**. He hasn't been able to wash the powder out of some of his clothing.

3 Write a paragraph describing a celebration, festival, or party using the words from Exercise 1 and your own information.

<u>We celebrated my grandparent's 40th anniversary recently. The dancing at their party was surprisingly lively! My uncle led off with a traditional song . . .</u>

_____

_____

_____

_____

_____

_____

_____

GRAMMAR -ing form (gerund) as subject; by/for + -ing form

1 How is the *-ing* form used? Read the sentences and check (✓) the correct columns.

	As the subject	To show how to do something	To show the purpose or use of something
1. **Decorating** the house for parties is my favorite part of the holidays.	✓		
2. The annual parade is an occasion for **wearing** silly hats.			
3. Not **bringing** a gift to the party would be rude.			
4. **Watching** the fireworks by the river is stunning.			
5. We began the ceremony by **singing** a song.			
6. The rainy weather isn't good for **watching** the parade.			

2 Correct the mistakes.

1. The park is perfect ~~by have~~ *for having* a picnic.
2. They celebrated their anniversary for take a long cruise.
3. One of Carrie's favorite things is for watches the leaves change color in the fall.
4. He improved his test scores to study every day.
5. My grandmother's kitchen is perfect by prepares food.
6. I tell everyone that for go to the Art Festival was the highlight of my trip.

3 Complete the conversation with the gerund forms of the verbs in parentheses. Add *by* or *for*, if necessary.

Maria: What was that festival you went to in December?

Kevin: I went to the Chocolate Festival. It's the perfect festival ¹ *for learning* (learn) about different types of chocolate.

Maria: That must be helpful since you're in culinary school, right? ² _____ (go) to the festival, you're learning something new. It's like studying for you!

Kevin: It really is. You get a sense of the variety of chocolate ³ _____ (taste) a lot of different kinds.

Maria: Oh, yeah! ⁴ _____ (no eat) as many kinds as you can would be a mistake!

Kevin: And the festival is not just about flavor. ⁵ _____ (watch) how chocolates are made is important, too.

Maria: I've heard that ⁶ _____ (make) chocolates is difficult.

Kevin: It is. ⁷ _____ (take) photos of the demonstrations has been a great way to take notes on the process.

Maria: Well, I can't wait to see what you've learned!

4 Write two sentences for each gerund phrase: one using *by* and one using *for*. Use your own ideas.

1. watch a concert

   by: *I started my weekend by watching a concert on TV.*

   for: *The outdoor theater in the park is great for watching a concert.*

   by: _____

   for: _____

2. play music

   by: _____

   for: _____

3. have a party

   by: _____

   for: _____

4. go to a festival

   by: _____

   for: _____

CONVERSATION Exclamations

1. Complete the conversation.

Great idea!	That'd be
How	That's such an
is so	~~What a~~

Josh: Hi, Lynn. I'm planning a birthday party for Glenn. I don't know what to do!

Lynn: ¹ _What a_ nice thing to do! I'll help you. Does he know about the party or is it a surprise party?

Josh: Hey! A surprise party! ² _____ Let's do that.

Lynn: Why don't we have it at your place? That way it can be a surprise.

Josh: ³ _____ smart of you to think of that! But I'm not sure about keeping it a surprise.

Lynn: Here's what you do: You pick him up to take him out for his birthday. Then you pretend to forget something at your house. Invite him in for a minute when you go back to get it. When he comes in, surprise!

Josh: ⁴ _____ perfect! OK. What else do we need to do?

Lynn: He ⁵ _____ into music. We'll need to make a really good playlist.

Josh: Very true. I can do that. Do we need to prepare food?

Lynn: Of course, and we'll need a cake.

Josh: Right! The cake! I almost forgot! ⁶ _____ important part of a birthday!

Lynn: Totally. Oh, I have a great idea! We can get one of those cakes with a photograph on it, done in frosting!

Josh: He'd like that.

2 Circle the correct answers.

1. **A:** I think for our school dance this winter, we should get an ice sculpture!
   B: **Great idea!** / **That'd be difficult.** But won't it be expensive?

2. **A:** Let's take Mike to a concert instead of throwing him a party.
   B: **How** / **What a** great idea! It'll feel like a huge party.

3. **A:** Melanie's favorite color is green. We can serve all green foods and drinks at the party!
   B: **How** / **Is so** cool! Oh, as long as it's not all vegetables!

4. **A:** Instead of having music at the party, I thought we'd sing karaoke.
   B: **That'd be** / **Is so** a good idea, except that Chris doesn't like singing!

5. **A:** What can I do to help with the class trip?
   B: Well, the trip **how** / **is so** expensive. We need to come up with ideas to raise money for it.

6. **A:** We're renting go-karts for Belinda's birthday next month!
   B: **How** / **That's such** a fun idea.

48 | Unit 7

READING TO WRITE

1 Jennifer started a company that plans parties. Complete Jennifer's email to her friend Craig. Write *so* or *too*.

To: CraigD@cup.net
From: JenniferLee@email.net
Subject: Too Fun!

Dear Craig,

I'm ¹ _so_ excited to tell you about how my party-planning company, Too Fun!, is doing. As you know, I started by planning my high school's graduation party. A lot of people think planning a party is a lot of work, but I don't. I love it. I like it when I have so much to do that I'm almost ² _____ busy to get it all done. We held the graduation in the school auditorium. We had an old-fashioned carnival theme, with games, prizes, and fun foods that people used to eat a long time ago. People took photos and had a great time.

Next, I planned my cousin's wedding reception. She paid me for it. It was ³ _____ luxurious! I rented a gorgeous inn along the coast. It was ⁴ _____ stunning. I hired a chef to prepare all of the couple's favorite foods. I planned for ⁵ _____ much food, though! We had a lot left over. But my cousin wasn't mad that I spent ⁶ _____ much on food. She was ⁷ _____ happy about her special day to care.

The next party I'm planning is a birthday party for our neighbor's daughter. I think I'm going to rent a pony! The pictures are going to be ⁸ _____ cute! I can just imagine it now.

How are things with you? Got any plans for your college graduation party? Let me know if you need any help!

Take care,

Jennifer

---

2 Read the email in Exercise 1 again. Answer the questions.

1. What two events did Jennifer plan?

   Event 1: _her high school's graduation party_

   Event 2: _____.

2. Where was each party held?

   Party 1: _____

   Party 2: _____

3. What did Jennifer have at each party?

   Party 1: _____

   Party 2: _____

4. What happened at each party?

   Party 1: _____

   Party 2: _____

5. What party is Jennifer planning next?

   _____

6. What will be special about the next party?

   _____

8 Mysteries and Secrets

VOCABULARY Adjectives with un-

1 Complete the puzzle.

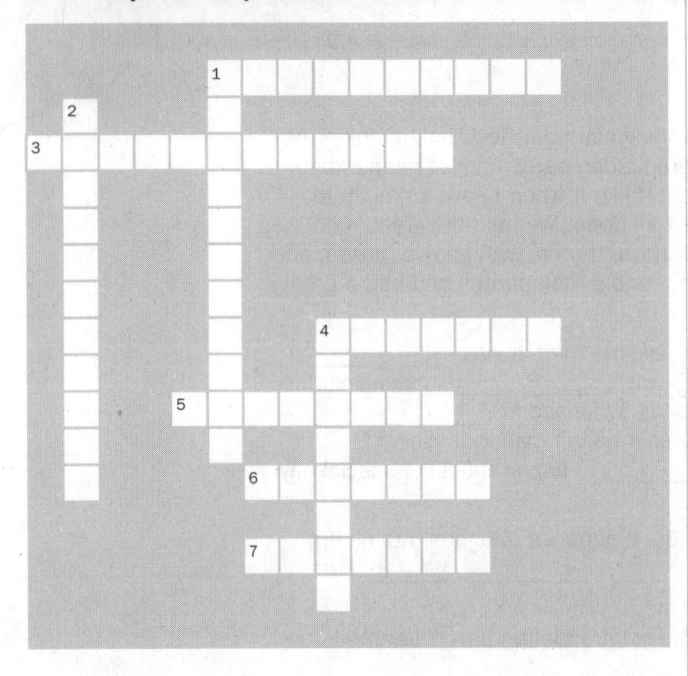

Across
1. Something that you don't know is going to happen is _____.
3. Something that doesn't seem true is _____.
4. Something that doesn't happen most of the time is _____.
5. If you don't find an answer to a problem or mystery, it is _____.
6. Something that isn't recognized by most people is _____.
7. When bad things happen to you a lot, you are _____.

Down
1. Something that is not valuable or useful is _____.
2. Something that isn't needed is _____.
4. When something probably won't happen it is _____.

2 Complete the sentences with some of the words from Exercise 1. More than one answer may be correct.

1. Mysterious crop circles appeared in the farmer's field. People came up with some pretty _____ explanations, like aliens caused the circles. But it turns out they were caused by an insect that makes an _____ pattern in the ground.

2. My brother is afraid he'll get bitten by a shark even though it's very _____. Very few people get bitten, so I think worrying about it is _____.

3. What happened to pilot Amelia Earhart is still an _____ mystery. But someone may have found a piece of her plane.

4. The reporter said that Banksy is a famous graffiti artist, but his real name and identity are _____. The reporter tried to discover the artist's true identity, but was _____ in his efforts to learn the truth.

5. A detective has to be careful when she looks for clues. A fingerprint or piece of hair that might seem small and _____ could turn out to be a big clue. And sometimes clues are found in _____ places, like on the backs of paintings or in the refrigerator!

3 Answer the questions with your own information.

1. Describe a time you felt unlucky.

   _____
   _____

2. Describe a time something unexpected happened to you or someone you know.

   _____
   _____

3. Describe something that you think is unbelievable.

   _____
   _____

4. Describe something that you think is unlikely to happen to you.

   _____
   _____

GRAMMAR Time clauses; present participle clauses

1 Use the chart to write sentences. Use the correct forms of the verbs. More than one answer may be possible.

Time clause	First event	Second event
1. before	Ben graduated.	He became a firefighter.
2. after	We had lived in the city for years.	We discovered our favorite restaurant.
3. when	They scored the final goal.	Helen arrived at the game.
4. when	I have enough money.	I will visit the Great Wall of China
5. before	It got dark out.	The fireworks started.

1. *Ben graduated before he became a firefighter.*
2. _____
3. _____
4. _____
5. _____

2 Complete the sentences about each pair of pictures with the correct time clauses. More than one answer may be possible.

1. She put on her helmet __*before*__ she went skateboarding.

2. Tina started taking photos _____ she got off the bus.

3. We saw dolphins in the river _____ our boat first left Iquitos, Peru.

4. We weren't scared _____ the bats came flying out of the cave!

3 Circle the correct answers.

1. Anna loved sushi **(as soon as)** / **until** she tried it.

2. José had booked his ticket to New Orleans **before** / **until** the hurricane hit. So he had to change his flight.

3. They will continue the space flight program **after** / **while** they have solved the problem.

4. Logan doesn't want to be in Chiang Mai **before** / **while** it's typhoon season.

5. The butterflies were arriving **after** / **when** the film crew was in Mexico, so they got great videos.

6. I had sore feet **before** / **after** I got my new running shoes. They are so much better than my old ones!

4 Write sentences that are true for you using time clauses. Use the words given.

1. since

   I've been interested in sharks since I was five.

   _____

2. before

   _____

3. when

   _____

4. after

   _____

VOCABULARY Reporting verbs

1 Circle the word that best replaces the underlined words.

1. Terry <u>told me</u> that there would be a surprise test on Tuesday. She did not explain how she knew that.
   a. agreed   b. **(claimed)**   c. recommended

2. By the way, when I spoke with him, Aaron <u>said</u> that he'd be studying at the library tonight.
   a. wrote   b. mentioned   c. insisted

3. My aunt finally <u>answered</u> my email asking about our family's history.
   a. replied to
   b. recommended to
   c. decided on

4. Charlotte <u>liked</u> my plan to start a book club. We're going to do it!
   a. recommended to
   b. admitted to
   c. agreed on

5. I wanted Chinese food and my sister wanted sushi, but my father <u>said</u> that we were going to get pizza for dinner.
   a. admitted   b. replied   c. decided

6. My friend <u>told me to read</u> Stephen King's novels. She thinks I'd like them.
   a. wrote   b. agreed   c. recommended

7. I knew my little brother drew on the wall, even though he wouldn't <u>say that he did</u>.
   a. admit it   b. recommend it   c. decide it

8. My mom <u>said</u> that I should clean the garage before watching TV.
   a. replied   b. claimed   c. insisted

9. The reporter <u>said in the article</u> that the mystery was solved. But the police chief didn't agree.
   a. admitted   b. agreed   c. wrote

2 Complete the sentences with the correct forms of the verbs.

admit	decide	recommend
agree	insist	reply
claim	~~mention~~	write

Alex: Hey, Bill. What's the matter?

Bill: What? Nothing! Did Haley ¹___mention___ something to you? She sent you over here, didn't she?

Alex: OK. I'll ²_____ it! She ³_____ that I find out what you're going to do.

Bill: I knew it! She ⁴_____ she doesn't mind if I run for student council against her. But I know she does mind.

Alex: I think you're right. It's just, she's upset because you ⁵_____ to run without talking to her first. It's weird to run against a close friend.

Bill: You know, I ⁶_____ it seems that way. I really do.

Alex: Well then, why did you do it?

Bill: Mr. Wells, my Political Science teacher, said it would help my college applications. He ⁷_____ that I do some extracurricular activities in school, like student council.

Alex: So, you'd ruin a friendship because you want a teacher to ⁸_____ a recommendation for you?

Bill: I hadn't really thought of it that way. But then again, if Haley is a good friend, she should understand. And, if she wants to work in politics, well, she'll have to get used to some friendly competition.

Alex: So, what should I tell her?

Bill: You don't have to talk to her about it. I'll ⁹_____ to her in person.

52 | Unit 8

3 Answer the questions using your own information.

1. Explain something important that you decided recently.

   _____

2. What is something your parents insist that you do?

   _____

3. What book, movie, or TV show do you recommend to people the most?

   _____

GRAMMAR Reported speech

1 Match the quoted speech to the reported speech.

1. She said, "Yes, I hid it in the garage."
2. He said, "I heard a strange sound around midnight."
3. He said, "Go look in the attic."
4. She asked, "Did you see anything odd?"
5. She said, "We have to leave the light on at night."
6. He said, "I was at home the entire evening."

a. He said that he was at home the entire evening.
b. She asked me if I saw anything odd.
c. She admitted to hiding it in the garage.
d. He claimed to hear a strange sound around midnight.
e. He told me to look in the attic.
f. She insisted on leaving the light on at night.

2 Change the direct speech to reported speech. Use the subjects and verb forms in parentheses.

1. "Hide the new puppy in Damian's room." (Mom / say)

   Mom said to hide the new puppy in Damian's room.

2. "Pretend you didn't see anything." (she / recommend)

   _____

3. "We'll meet at the old clock." (we / agree)

   _____

4. "Where were you on the night of January 7?" (he / ask)

   _____

5. "Tim is hiding under the bed." (she / admit)

   _____

6. "I know who did it." (he / insist on)

   _____

Indirect questions

3 Read the indirect questions. Write the direct questions.

1. I wonder where the treasure is hidden.

   "Where is the treasure hidden?"

2. I don't know why he recommended telling her the secret.

   _____

3. Can you tell me why he said not to tell anyone?

   _____

4. I wonder if she asked why he did it.

   _____

4 Read the conversation. Rewrite the police officer's questions as indirect questions. Then rewrite the detective's answers as reported speech. Use the words in parentheses.

Detective: What was she doing when her bag was stolen?
Police officer: She was eating lunch.
Detective: Did she see anyone take it?
Police officer: No, she didn't.
Detective: Where was her bag sitting?
Police officer: It was hanging on the back of her chair.

1. **Detective:** *Can you tell me what she was doing when her bag was stolen?*
2. **Police officer:** _____ (said)
3. **Detective:** _____ (wonder)
4. **Police officer:** _____ (claimed)
5. **Detective:** _____ (tell)
6. **Police officer:** _____ (mention)

CONVERSATION Confirming and denying

1. **Put the words in the correct order to make sentences.**

   1. **A:** / is / invention / say / Richard Branson / that / people / interested in / Some / buying / your / !

      Some people say that Richard Branson is interested in buying your invention!

      B: absolutely / Yes, / !

      _____

   3. **A:** / you / Is / were / attacked / true / by / a / it / shark / that / ?

      _____

      B: all / Not / at / !

      _____

   5. **A:** your / profits / comment / on / you / Can / ?

      _____

      B: joking / must / You / be / !

      _____

2. **Complete the conversation with the sentences from Exercise 1.**

   Dana: I'm interviewing Sam Logan. He invented a boat that you pedal and steer like a car. Sam, what was your inspiration for this invention?

   Sam: I really like boats and bicycling. So I thought I'd put them together. I was surprised when it worked!

   Dana: Sam has produced and sold about 125 of these so far. So, Sam, that seems like a lot to sell.

   1 _____

   Sam: Well, Dana. They cost a lot to make, so really, I don't make much on each one. It's just fun for me.

   Dana: 2 _____ Is that true?

   Sam: 3 _____
   That's funny! I haven't heard from him. But if he does, I will make him a special one!

   Dana: It seems like this could be dangerous.
   4 _____

   Sam: 5 _____
   That's just a story someone made up! I've never seen any swimming out here. I think the vehicle is kind of large and would scare them.

   Dana: Last question, can I take it for a spin?

   Sam: 6 _____
   Here, let me show you how to drive it . . .

54 | Unit 8

READING TO WRITE

1 Complete the sentences with the correct phrases.

but I'd also   in order to   not only   so that

1. The thief had to be very quiet _____ not set off the alarms.

2. The thief lied _____ the detective wouldn't think he stole the jewelry.

3. "_____ did I know the thief was lying, _____ guessed where he hid the jewels," said the detective.

2 Complete the text with the phrases from Exercise 1.

MY SECRET

by Harry Sykes

I have a younger brother named Carl. When he was five and I was nine, we used to share the same bedroom. His bedtime was before mine. He would still sleep with his favorite teddy bear in those days. And every night, when I came to bed, I would place his other stuffed animals on his bed. ¹_____ would I put them in there, ²_____ dress them up in his clothing. I had to be very quiet ³_____ not wake him up.

Every morning, he'd wake up to find his stuffed animals wearing his clothing. He thought they got dressed during the night! Then I'd act surprised ⁴_____ he wouldn't suspect I did it. Finally, at breakfast, he'd tell my mother what clothes the toys were wearing. She thought he was making it all up! To this day, I've never admitted what I'd done.

3 Read the text again. Answer the questions.

1. What is the story about?
   _____

2. What is the background information?
   Who: _____
   Where: _____
   When: _____

3. What is the order of events?
   First: _____
   Next: _____
   Then: _____
   Last: _____

4. How does the story conclude?
   _____

REVIEW UNITS 7–8

1 Cross out the word that doesn't belong in each category.

1. **Preparing for a party:**
   ~~admit something~~   prepare special food
   dress up   put up decorations

2. **Celebrating:**
   write a report   have a good time
   hold a contest   set off fireworks

3. **Describing a party:**
   crowded   lively   reply   noisy

4. **Describing how people say things:**
   admit   claim   recommend   unsolved

2 Circle the correct words.

1. Juanita **admitted** / **claimed** to telling him about the surprise party.
2. Boris **mentioned** / **insisted** on driving us home after the celebration.
3. Luisa **agreed** / **wrote** to me that the party was a huge success.
4. Amy **agreed** / **told** to help me put up decorations before the party.
5. Ted **recommended** / **replied** to her question by email.

3 Write the quoted speech as reported speech. Use the words in parentheses.

1. Jill: "I told them about the contest." (claim)
   Jill claimed she told them about the contest.

2. Mark: "OK. I'll help you choose some music to play at the party." (agree)
   _____
   _____

3. Brandon: "You're coming to the party!" (insist)
   _____
   _____

4. Olga: "The food at the school festival was pretty good." (say)
   _____
   _____

5. Evan: "I saw them dancing at the party." (mention)
   _____
   _____

4 Complete the text with the correct words.

colorful	messy	~~traditional~~
crowded	noisy	unusual
lively	stunning	

Throw a Great Party!

We asked some teens for ideas on how to make your next party an event to remember. Here's what they said:

- **Alex:** ᵃFood is key to having a great event. Serve ¹ _traditional_ foods, like sushi, but arrange them in an ² _____ way, for example, to look like a nature scene or a funny face the stranger the better! ᵇRemember to have napkins in case things get ³ _____!

- **Tracy:** ᶜPlay ⁴ _____ music to get people dancing! ᵈMove the furniture out of the way so the room doesn't feel ⁵ _____. You'll know everyone is having fun when it's so ⁶ _____ you have to talk loudly to be heard over the party!

- **Tom:** ᵉHold a contest! ᶠI really enjoy singing contests. Award a prize for the most ⁷ _____ performance. Or make it a costume party. Encourage people to get crazy with their costumes by offering a prize for the brightest and most ⁸ _____ costume.

5 Write the lettered sentences from the text in Activity 4 as reported speech.

a. Alex said _that food is key to having a great event_.
b. He also said that _____.
c. Tracy said to _____.
d. She also recommends
   _____.
e. Tom suggests _____.
f. He said that _____.

6 Complete the conversations. Use verb + -ing form or infinitive.

1. **A:** I don't know what to do for my birthday.
   B: I'd _consider having_ (consider / have) a theme party.
2. **A:** I'm working on the invitation list for my wedding.
   B: Don't _____ (forget / send) them early.
3. **A:** I'm not sure where to have our company party.
   B: If you _____ (decide / have) the party at a restaurant, be sure to call early for a reservation.
4. **A:** I'm planning a karaoke party for my parents!
   B: Not everybody _____ (enjoy / sing) karaoke.
5. **A:** What did you get Jeff for his birthday?
   B: I _____ (try / get) him concert tickets, but they were sold out.

7 Correct the sentences.

1. Before ~~released~~ _releasing_ the official report, the police wanted to make sure it was final.
2. When the detective will have all the facts, she'll reveal who committed the crime.
3. If you look at the map since you go, you won't get lost.
4. After to hide the prize money, the millionaire posted clues on his website so people could try to find it.
5. Jenna always reads the end of the mystery since she finishes the book.
6. Before they made the discovery, they shared their results with other scientists.

8 Complete the conversation.

am so	Not at all!	You must be joking!
Great idea!	That's such a	
~~Is it true that~~	Yes, absolutely!	

Erin: Hey, Russ. ¹ _Is it true that_ you had a huge party last weekend?

Russ: ² _____
I was studying for my lifeguard test all weekend!

Erin: I was just kidding. But have you heard that I'm planning a big graduation party?

Russ: No way! ³ _____
How do you have time to plan a party with finals coming up?

Erin: I find the time because I want to do it! So get this, our whole class is invited. It'll be a three-day camping trip!

Russ: ⁴ _____
Camping is awesome.

Erin: I know. I
⁵ _____
excited. It's going to be at the lake. Can you be our lifeguard?

Russ: ⁶ _____
I'd be happy to.
⁷ _____
great spot to camp.

Erin: Yeah!

9 Weird and Wonderful

VOCABULARY Story elements

1 Find seven more story element words.

O	X	W	G	Z	C	P	M	D	K	S	X	Q	T
B	Z	I	R	A	U	F	M	I	U	R	I	V	E
F	D	D	T	W	W	G	B	J	L	D	R	S	N
M	W	A	V	H	H	Q	V	C	F	S	J	E	D
R	F	O	G	V	L	G	O	F	W	E	I	X	I
M	A	I	N	C	H	A	R	A	C	T	E	R	N
P	Y	C	M	Z	V	Y	U	I	Z	T	T	C	G
E	B	Z	P	A	O	X	A	C	T	I	O	N	F
G	V	I	L	L	A	I	N	R	G	N	G	H	P
D	F	P	L	T	T	G	D	L	C	G	E	W	Q
B	H	G	K	X	Q	S	A	M	H	M	N	L	C
A	N	A	D	W	(P	L	O	T)	Y	B	I	D	K
L	U	O	E	H	E	R	O	M	G	I	Q	Q	R
H	L	W	S	U	S	P	E	N	S	E	K	C	B

2 Replace the underlined phrases with the words and phrases from Exercise 1. Some words will be used more than once.

1. Brenda thinks the *Harry Potter* movies do a good job of keeping the story the same and not changing the ~~things that happened~~. *plot*

2. The book series *Percy Jackson and the Olympians* is named after the important person in the story, Percy Jackson, so we know the books are about him.

3. When they made the movie *Jurassic Park*, they changed the last part of the story from how it was in the book.

4. Tim likes fantasy movies like *The Hobbit* because he likes the place where and when the story happens.

5. Darth Vader, President Coriolanus Snow, and the Joker, are all examples of the bad person in a story.

6. Luke Skywalker, Katniss Everdeen, and Batman are all examples of the good person in a story.

7. Angela wouldn't watch the movie *Jaws* because the feeling of excitement when something is about to happen was too much for her! She said it made her nervous.

8. *Indiana Jones and the Raiders of the Lost Ark* is one of Bill's favorite movies. He loves watching movies with a lot of exciting things happening.

3 Complete the sentences with your own information.

1. My favorite hero in a story is *Spider Man* because *I think it's cool the way he had to learn about power himself.*
   My favorite hero in a story is _____ because _____.

2. My favorite villain in a story is _____ because _____.

3. I don't like it when the main character is _____ because _____.

4. I liked the action in the story _____ because _____.

5. I think the story with the best setting is _____ because _____.

GRAMMAR Third conditional

1 Write third conditional sentences with the information in the chart.

	Imaginary and untrue situation in the past	Impossible consequence
1.	Lesley / not save / the money	she / not buy / a car
2.	You / study	you / do better / on your test than me
3.	Carl / not hear / the noise	he / not lock / the door
4.	Karen and Cindy / not take / photos	no one / believe / their story
5.	Max / go / the beach	he / compete / the swimming contest
6.	I / be nice / to my coach	I / get / more help

1. *If Lesley hadn't saved the money, she wouldn't have bought a car.*
2. _____
3. _____
4. _____
5. _____
6. _____

2 Write the questions another way. Then answer the questions with your own information.

1. What would've happened if you had won a million dollars last year?

   Q: *If you had won a million dollars last year, what would've happened?*

   A: *I would have traveled around the world.*

2. What kind of movie would it have been if you had been in a movie?

   Q: _____

   A: _____

3. If you had helped a friend last year, who would you have helped?

   Q: _____

   A: _____

4. What celebrity would you have invited if you had had a big birthday party last year?

   Q: _____

   A: _____

5. If you had known what it would be like, what movie wouldn't you have watched?

   Q: _____

   A: _____

wish + past perfect

3 Put the words in the correct order to make sentences using wish + past perfect.

1. I / I / for / test / wish / studied / the / had / .

   I wish I had studied for the test.

2. gotten / I / sooner / had / wish / I / up / .

   _____

3. run / wishes / had / the / Mike / race / faster / he / in / .

   _____

4. gotten / Kim / had / she / wishes / concert / tickets / .

   _____

5. before / had / we / We / it / rained / left / wish / .

   _____

6. movie / hadn't / wish / heard / how / we / the / ended / We / .

   _____

VOCABULARY Linking phrases

1 Complete the sentences with a word or phrase from each box.

according	again
as a	course
in	fact
in	order to
of	result of
rather	than
so	that
then	to

1. Stephen King was signing books at the bookstore. ___Of course___, I asked him to sign my copy of his book.
2. Jeanne moved to Hollywood _____ become a movie star.
3. Jonah thought it would be cool to see a ghost, but _____, maybe it wouldn't.
4. Leon could never get to the airport on time, so he bought his own plane _____ miss any more flights.
5. They held the wedding in secret _____ photographers wouldn't spoil their special day.
6. For a long time, Pluto was classified as a planet, when _____, it was really a "dwarf" planet.
7. _____ recent research, the Earth and Moon are 60 million years older than previously thought.
8. She's studied Chinese for years and _____ her studies, she speaks it very well now.

2 Put the words in the correct order to make sentences.

1. visit / most interesting / my friend Juan, / place / Macchu Picchu/ According to / is / the / to / .
   According to my friend Juan, Macchu Picchu
   is the most interesting place to visit.

2. tomato / The / is considered a vegetable, / in / a fruit / fact, / it's / but / .
   _____
3. formed / result / the hoodoos / of / As a / snow and rain, / were / .
   _____
4. all / I / marine animals / love / .
   I / swim / with / Of / wouldn't / a shark / want to / course, / !
   _____
   _____
5. movie / video camera / in / to / make / order / John / is / buying / a / a / .
   _____
6. saved / she / money / could / that / Helen / go / college / to / so / .
   _____
7. than / we / a trip / Bryce Canyon, / Rather / took / there / about / just read / .
   _____

GRAMMAR Past modals of speculation

1 Read the sentences. Is the speaker sure or not sure? Check (✓) the correct columns.

	Sure	Not sure
1. Jorge must have been to Mexico City before.	✓	
2. His younger brother couldn't have learned to drive already.		
3. We may have been the first people to see the cave.		
4. Iris might have been at the dance last night.		
5. Henry must not have known that the show was canceled.		
6. They might not have seen this movie before.		

2 Match the statements with the correct speculations.

1. Liam wasn't home last night. __b__	a. He must have worked hard on it.
2. Tomás didn't go to the free concert last weekend. ____	b. He could have been at his grandmother's.
3. Albert didn't answer his phone. ____	c. He couldn't have completed all of the levels yet.
4. Erik's movie won the school video contest. ____	d. He might have turned it off.
5. Min-Jun got a new car. ____	e. He must not have known about it.
6. Eduard just got that new video game. ____	f. He must be so excited.

3 Complete the sentences. Use the modals in parentheses and *have* + past participle.

1. Anna was out in the rain. She <u>must not have brought</u> (must not / bring) her umbrella.

2. Paul is tired today. He _____ (might / go) to bed late.

3. Joel didn't ride the roller coaster. He _____ (may / be) too scared.

4. Nicole's car has a flat tire. She _____ (could not / drive) to work today.

5. Alec didn't mention how his band's audition went. It _____ (may not / go) very well.

6. Jin-hee can't find her cat. But it _____ (might not / run) away.

4 Rewrite the sentences. Use the modals in parentheses and *have* + past participle.

1. Abby was worried about the test. (could)
   Abby could have been worried about the test.

2. They didn't eat dessert. (must not)
   _____

3. Greg went to the play by himself. (might)
   _____

4. We didn't get good seats in the theater. (could not)
   _____

5. Scientists know why the bees are dying. (must)
   _____

6. I lost my friend's necklace. (may)
   _____

CONVERSATION — Asking for more information

1. Put the words in the correct order to make sentences and questions.

1. about / Tell / me / it / .
   Tell me about it.

2. happened / What / next / ?
   _____

3. that / Why / was / ?
   _____

4. happened / what / So, / ?
   _____

5. what / next / brilliant / And / then / he / did / was / !
   _____

6. kind / of / what / business / Like / ?
   _____

2 Complete the conversation with the expressions from Exercise 1. More than one answer may be possible.

Jack: I read this really interesting story about Richard Branson last night.

Marnie: Richard Branson, the British businessman? The guy who started Virgin Airlines?
¹ *Tell me about it.*

Jack: Yeah, it's such an amazing story how he started an airline. He was in his late 20s and he had already started one business.

Marnie: ² _____

Jack: It was a business that sold records. He started it in 1972, and it was called Virgin Records. Anyway, one night, he was going to fly to the Virgin Islands in the Caribbean. But his flight was canceled. So he was stuck at the airport.

Marnie: ³ _____

Jack: Because there weren't any more flights that night. But he had to get to the Virgin Islands.

Marnie: ⁴ _____

Jack: He found a private plane that he could "charter," or rent. But he didn't have the money to charter it.

Marnie: ⁵ _____

Jack: He chartered the plane anyway!
⁶ _____
He made a sign that said "Virgin Airlines, $39." And he sold the other seats on the plane to the other passengers who would have been on his canceled flight. After that, he bought the plane!

62 | Unit 9

READING TO WRITE

1 Complete Cesar's story with the adverbs in the box. Sometimes more than one answer is possible.

clearly	Luckily
~~Eventually~~	Obviously
finally	Suddenly
Finally	Unfortunately
fortunately	

The Robot Competition
by Cesar Guerrero

Last weekend, my friend Hiro and I entered a robot in my town's robot competition. We had worked on it for a year. ¹ _Eventually_, it was ready to enter in the contest.

In the competition, each robot got a turn in front of the judges. You had to show what your robot could do. Hiro and I thought our robot was ² _____ the best.

We waited and waited for our turn. The judges ³ _____ called our names. Hiro used the remote control to make our robot move. It walked, it spun, it punched. ⁴ _____, the robot did everything Hiro commanded it to do. Then I took the controls and made the robot dance. The robot ⁵ _____ did everything I wanted it to. ⁶ _____, we were very proud of our robot. When our turn was finished, Hiro and I thought we were going to win!

⁷ _____, the judges couldn't decide! There was a tie between our robot and another robot. The judges made us perform one more time.

I took the controls and started to make the robot dance. ⁸ _____, the robot started to do different things. For several minutes, I tried to make it dance again, but it wouldn't respond to the controls. ⁹ _____, it rolled right off the table. Hiro and I lost the competition!

2 Read the story in Exercise 1 again. Look at the adverbs you wrote. Circle the words that show time, underline the words that show opinion, and put a box around the words that state a fact.

3 Read the story in Exercise 1 again. Circle the correct answers.

1. What happens first in the story?
   a. The boys enter their robot in a competition. *(circled)*
   b. The boys become judges.
   c. The boys learn how to make a robot.

2. When did the story happen?
   a. two years ago
   b. last month
   c. last weekend

3. Where did the story happen?
   a. at a robot competition
   b. at a robot club
   c. at a friend's house

4. What happened first?
   a. The robot suddenly stopped working.
   b. Cesar controlled the robot.
   c. The robot performed well.

5. What happened next?
   a. Cesar got mad at Hiro.
   b. Cesar broke the robot.
   c. The robot couldn't be controlled.

6. What happened at the end of the story?
   a. Cesar and Hiro won the competition.
   b. Cesar and Hiro lost the competition.
   c. Cesar and Hiro quit competing.

10 I Have To! I Can!

VOCABULARY Training and qualifications

1 Write the collocations. Use a word from each box.

application	course
application	degree
career	exam
college	experience
entrance	fees
training	form
work	path

1. You fill this out to get a job. *application form*
2. This program teaches you the skills you need to do a job. _____
3. You take this test to get into a college or university. _____
4. After you graduate from college, you earn one of these. _____
5. A summer job or internship to gain familiarity with the kind of career you want is this. _____
6. When you apply to get into colleges, you often have to pay these. _____
7. This is a series of steps leading to a desired job. _____

2 Write the phrases from Exercise 1 in the correct categories. Some may be used more than once.

1. **Things you needed to get into a college or university:**

   _____application form_____,
   _____,
   _____

2. **Things you might need to get a job:**

   _____,
   _____

3. **Things that can make up your career path:**

   _____,
   _____

3 Complete the sentences with some of the phrases from Exercise 1.

1. Miranda had to report all her grades and test scores as part of her _____.
2. Dean was surprised that he had to take an _____ for his local college.
3. Nadine knew that gaining _____ in local politics would look good on her résumé.
4. Kim decided not to pursue a _____ and instead started her own company. She wanted to follow a different _____ from her friends.
5. Genevieve was surprised that the _____ required to become a veterinary technician was almost as long as getting a college degree.
6. Joel only applied to his top-three universities because he didn't want to pay any additional _____.

4 Answer the questions with your own information.

1. Do you want to get a college degree or go through a training course? Why?

   _____
   _____

2. What kind of work experience do you need for your career path?

   _____
   _____

3. What do you think of entrance exams?

   _____
   _____

4. Have you ever paid application fees?

   _____

GRAMMAR Past ability

1 Circle the correct words. Then match the questions with the correct responses.

1. **Could** / **Did** he **able to read** / **read** when he was three? _c_
2. **Was** / **Were** she **able to** / **managed to** take the entrance exam last weekend? ___
3. How **did** / **was** he **could** / **manage** to graduate from high school early? ___
4. What **could** / **managed** she **do** / **to do** at 12? ___
5. **Could** / **Did** he **able to** / **manage to** get the job? ___

a. He **could** / **managed to take** extra classes.
b. She **could** / **able to** speak Russian.
c. Yes, he **able to read** / **could read** simple books.
d. No, he **didn't** / **wasn't**. He didn't have enough work experience.
e. Yes, she **was** / **were**.

2 Put the words in the correct order to make sentences and questions.

1. college / you / summer / money / manage / to / enough / for / save / Did / this / ?

   Did you manage to save enough money for
   college this summer?

2. when / Karen / was / 18, / drive / couldn't / she / .

   _____

3. Cambridge / able / Yuri / to / How / get / accepted / to / was / ?

   _____

4. concert / didn't / manage / win / We / tickets / the / to / to / .

   _____

5. could / she / How / many / play / Nina / was / instruments / five / when / ?

   _____

6. the / they / to / at / able / conference / were / What / learn / ?

   _____

3 Look at Michael's activities. Complete questions about his past abilities using *could (not)*, *was/were able to*, and *managed to*. Then answer the questions.

played music (five instruments)	at age 10
earned money by making digital music and DJing; bought a car	at age 16
played at a famous music festival	one summer while still in school
studied music at a local college; created a music app for smartphones in spare time	after graduating from high school

1. ___Could___ Michael ___play music___ when he was young?

   ___Yes, he could play five instruments.___

2. How _____ he _____ buy a car at age 16?

   _____

3. What _____ he _____ one summer while he was still in school?

   _____

4. _____ he _____ study music after graduating from high school?

   _____

5. How _____ he _____ create a music app while studying music in college?

   _____

4 Answer the questions with your own information.

1. Could you drive when you were 10?

   _____

2. What could you do when you were nine?

   _____

3. Could you speak English very well last year?

   _____

4. What is the most difficult thing you've done? How did you manage to do it?

   _____

VOCABULARY Jobs

1 Look at the pictures and complete the crossword.

across
5.
7.
9.

down
1.
2.
3.
4.
6.
8.

2 Circle the correct answers.

1. Getting a law degree might be good for a career as **an athlete / a chef /(a politician)**.

2. My cousin is interested in law. He thinks he wants to be a **babysitter / designer / police officer**.

3. Miho loves shopping and clothes. She should just get a job as a **babysitter / politician / salesperson**.

4. Andy has worked at many restaurants over the years. Eventually, he became the head **chef / designer / musician** at a fancy restaurant.

5. When my sister turns 13, she wants to start to work as a **babysitter / police officer / politician**.

6. Arun is creative and has great style. He wants to be **an athlete / a designer / a police officer**.

7. Nancy is great at skiing. She hopes to become a professional **athlete / artist / salesperson**.

8. Graham got a job with the symphony as a **babysitter / musician / politician**. Instead of an entrance exam, he had to perform a solo.

9. My friend is a successful **artist / chef / salesperson**. You can see her work in the museum.

3 Answer the questions with words from Exercise 1 and your own ideas.

1. Which jobs might active people enjoy?
   _____
   _____

2. Which jobs might creative people enjoy?
   _____

3. Which jobs might people who like to work with other people enjoy?
   _____

4. Name a famous person for four different jobs:

Job	Name
Athlete	Cristiano Ronaldo

GRAMMAR Modal expressions for past and future

1 Match the questions with the answers.

1. Will you need a degree to be a politician? _e_	a. I'll need to take it by next November.
2. When will you need to take the entrance exam? ___	b. I had to talk to the manager and the owner of the company.
3. How often did you need to practice? ___	c. Yes, I will. But only for the first year.
4. Who did you have to talk to? ___	d. No, I didn't. But there was a fee to take the entrance exam.
5. Will you need to work on weekends? ___	e. No, I won't. But it would help.
6. Did you have to pay an application fee? ___	f. I needed to practice every day.

2 Circle the correct words.

Tara: Hi, Dan. Thanks for answering my questions about medical school. ¹**Did / Had** you ²**have to need / need to take** special classes in college before medical school?

Dan: Yes, I ³**did / had**. Everyone has to take pre-med. It's hard! It's a lot of chemistry, for one thing.

Tara: I've heard that. And what ⁴**did / would** you ⁵**have / have to do** to apply to medical school?

Dan: I ⁶**had to take / would take** the entrance exam. There's a special one for medical school. It's really hard.

Tara: Yeah? And what science classes ⁷**need / will** you ⁸**to take / have to take** when school starts in the fall?

Dan: I ⁹**will have to take / won't have to take** any!

Tara: What? Why?

Dan: Didn't my mom tell you? I got an offer from a soccer league! I can't turn that down! Looks like I ¹⁰**need to be / won't have to be** working on my soccer skills instead!

make and let

3 Complete the sentences with the correct form of make or let.

1. Our English teacher ____made____ us give speeches so we would be comfortable talking to people.

2. I offered to help, but my parents won't _____ me work at their shop. They want me to spend my time doing homework instead.

3. Sometimes I _____ my friends influence my opinions too much.

4. Tim's school _____ everyone wear uniforms, except on Fridays, when the school _____ students wear what they want.

5. I can't believe Ian _____ you cut his hair! How did you talk him into it?

6. That news program didn't _____ me very happy.

4 Answer the questions with your own information.

1. What is something your teacher makes you do?
   My teacher makes me rewrite every paper.

2. What is something parents usually make their young children do?
   _____

3. What is something you have to make yourself do?
   _____

4. What do your friend's parents let him or her do?
   _____

5. What is something your parents will let you do when you're older?
   _____

6. What do you wish your school would let you do?
   _____

CONVERSATION Making decisions

1 Match the phrases to make sentences.

1. How about _c_
2. Why ____
3. I've made up ____
4. That depends on ____
5. Ben might change his mind ____
6. Although, on second thought, ____

a. maybe we should make them see each other.
b. about coming on the hike.
c. going on a hike with him?
d. my mind.
e. the weather.
f. not?

2 Complete the conversation with the sentences from Exercise 1.

Doris: What should we do this weekend?

Frank: Ben is around this weekend. ¹ _How about going on a hike with him?_

Doris: ² _____
I heard it might rain. Also, I'm not sure about letting Ben coming with us.

Frank: ³ _____

Doris: Well, I told Sophia she could do something with us this weekend.

Frank: Oh, right. If Sophia's coming, ⁴ _____.

Doris: Yeah, he might. ⁵ _____ Then they'd have to get along.

Frank: I'm not sure that's a good idea.

Doris: You know what? ⁶ _____ I think we should have a big party. Then everyone will *have* to get along.

Frank: That might work.

Doris: Yeah, and if it doesn't, it might be interesting anyways!

68 | Unit 10

READING TO WRITE

1 Complete the sentences with *either . . . or* or *neither . . . nor*.

1. Jenny doesn't like peanut butter. And she doesn't like jelly.

   Jenny likes _____ peanut butter _____ jelly.

2. Misha wants to learn to play the violin. But if he can't play that, he'd be happy with piano.

   Misha wants to play _____ the violin _____ the piano.

2 Read the text. Then rewrite the underlined sentences using *either . . . or* or *neither . . . nor*.

Do you know Ella Marija Lani Yelich-O'Connor? Here's a hint: ¹She is not an actor. She is not a fashion designer. She's a singer. ²She is not from Australia. And she is not from the U.K. She's from New Zealand. She's under 25. Her stage name is one word. Guessed it yet?

If you guessed the pop singer Lorde, you're correct!

Lorde was interested in performing as a young girl. She was in drama school at the age of five. Her mother let her read all kinds of books as a child. When she was 13, her band won the school's talent show. When she was 15, she took singing lessons twice a week and also began writing songs. Eventually, she released a record, and the single "Royals" became a number-one hit in the United States in 2012, making Lorde the youngest singer to do that since 1988. Her debut album from 2013 was nominated for a Grammy Award. "Tennis Court" and "Glory and Gore" were hit songs from that album. She has also written songs for the *Hunger Games* movies soundtrack.

How does she sound? She doesn't play any instruments, so she uses her voice to carry the story of her songs. ³ So you could call her voice intriguing. Some says it's mysterious. What type of music is it? ⁴ I'd say her music is pop. Or it's electro. In 2013, *Time* magazine named her one of the most influential teenagers in the world. We can't wait to hear more from her!

1. _____
2. _____
3. _____
4. _____

3 Read the text again. Answer the questions.

1. What is Lorde's real name?

   _____

2. Where is she from?

   _____

3. What type of music does she play?

   _____

4. When and how did she start?

   _____

5. What are some of her hit songs?

   _____

6. What are some interesting facts about her?

   _____

REVIEW UNITS 9–10

1 Look at the pictures and complete the puzzle. Then use the words in grey to solve the riddle.

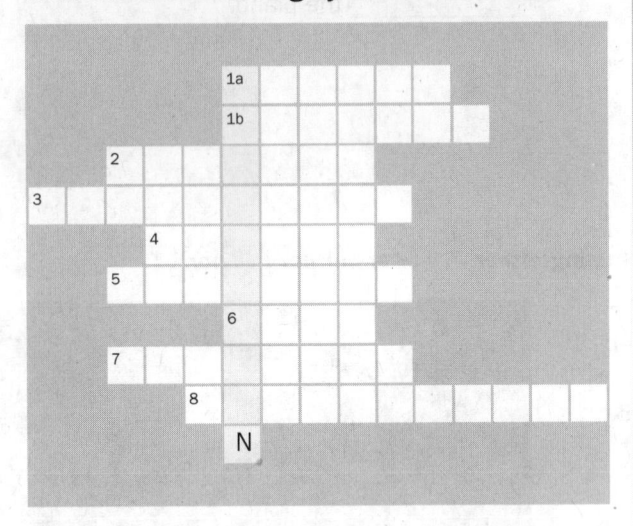

I am not an athlete, but I have to "run" for office. What job do I have?

1a. and 1b. (two words).

2 Put the words in the correct order to make sentences.

1. have / Soren / to / entrance / take / Did / an / exam / ?

   _____

2. work / get / did / need / you / experience / to / What / ?

   _____

3. will / take / Jun Hee / When / training / to / have / the / course / ?

   _____

4. application / Kelly / had / forms / to / fill / seven / out / .

   _____

5. degree / have / college / to / Will / earn / a / Josh / ?

   _____

6. didn't / I / to / path / on / need / a / career / decide / .

   _____

3 Complete the sentences with the correct forms of *let* or *make*.

1. Our boss doesn't _____ us fill out time sheets.

2. That training course we took last month _____ us see police officers in a new way.

3. My parents won't _____ me drive until I'm 18!

4. My parents _____ me play computer games as often as I like, as long as my grades are good.

4 Complete the article with the correct words.

According to	In fact
~~as a result of~~	Rather than
in order to	so that

Hope LeVin

Who is Hope LeVin? She's a professional athlete. She grew up in the Turks and Caicos Islands in the Caribbean. She used to watch kiteboarders on the beach when she was growing up.

When she was 11, someone asked her if she'd like to learn how. She said yes, and [1] *as a result* of that decision, she grew up to become a professional kiteboarder! [2] _____ being an overnight success, Hope had to work hard for many years. She kited every day, but for the first couple of months, she could only ride in one direction. She kept practicing [3] _____, eventually, she could ride in both directions. [4] _____ Hope, you have to be really patient [5] _____ learn kiteboarding.

In 2013, she entered a kiteboarding competition in the Dominican Republic. She didn't expect to do well, but [6] _____, she managed to win second place! That was when she decided to turn pro.

When Hope isn't kiting, competing, or spreading the word of kiteboarding, she's studying for a long-distance degree in economics. That's Hope LeVin, flying high!

5 Circle the correct words.

Lois: Hi Emi! Did you hear what happened to Carl?

Emi: No, ¹(tell me about it) / like what?

Lois: He went to the city and tried out for that reality show for musicians.

Emi: That's great! ²**So, what happened? / In fact?**

Lois: Well, he wasn't going to audition at all. But his friend Dylan, who's in his band, got him to ³**on second thought / change his mind**. So he went along with Dylan to the audition. He was thinking, ⁴"**Why was that / Why not** give it a try?" But then he said he almost didn't go through with it.

Emi: ⁵**On second thought. / Why was that?**

Lois: He said when they got there, there was only one spot left to audition. Dylan wanted it. And so did a bunch of other kids. They were all standing in line waiting to be chosen. So Carl ⁶**made up his mind / that depends on** that he'd let Dylan have the spot. And he went off to the side and just started listening to his headphones and dancing and singing to himself.

Emi: ⁷**And then what happened? / Like what?**

Lois: Well, one of the show's producers saw him dancing and singing to himself and she came over to him. She said, "⁸**How about / That depends on** if you take the last spot to audition?"

Emi: Oh my gosh! What did he do?

Lois: He said he looked over at Dylan and Dylan encouraged him, so he said yes! He's going to be on the show!

6 Read the conversation in Exercise 5 again. Imagine that Carl's audition was really a short story that Lois wrote. Answer the questions.

1. Who is the main character of the story?
   _____
2. What is the setting of the story?
   _____
3. In the story, was Dylan a hero, a villain, or neither? Why?
   _____
4. What was the plot of the story?
   _____
   _____
5. What happened at the end of the story?
   _____
   _____

7 Complete the sentences about Exercise 5. Use the words in parentheses to make the third conditional or past modals of speculation.

1. If Dylan hadn't invited him, Carl _wouldn't have gone to the audition_. (go /audition)
2. If Carl had stayed in line, _____. (might not / choose)
3. If Carl hadn't been singing and dancing on the side, the producer _____. (may not / notice)
4. But if Carl had stayed in line, he _____. (could not / be seen)
5. I bet Dylan _____ he _____ in line. (wish / had not / stay)
6. I wonder if Dylan _____ he _____ Carl to come to the audition! (wish / had not / ask)

Survival OBJECTS

Unit 6 Video 6.1

BEFORE YOU WATCH

1 Look at the pictures from the video and read the sentences. Write the letter of the correct definition of each underlined word.

1. The man fills his <u>parachute</u> with snow so he doesn't fall down the mountains. _____
2. He sleeps in a <u>cave</u> in the snow. _____
3. There can be <u>cracks</u> in the ice beneath the deep snow that are very dangerous. _____

a. a piece of equipment that allows a person to fall slowly through the air when dropped from an aircraft
b. a very narrow break or opening in something
c. a large hole in the ground or in a hill

WHILE YOU WATCH

2 Watch the video. Answer the questions.

1. Why does Bear have to be careful in the beginning of the video? _____
2. How does he make his snow cave? _____
3. How does he get water to drink? _____
4. How does he stay warm at night? _____
5. What does he have to do in the morning to find food and keep warm? _____

3 Watch the video again. Are the sentences true (*T*) or false (*F*)? Correct the false sentences.

1. Bear uses his backpack to dig in the snow. _____
2. During the night, Bear gets covered with water. _____
3. In the morning, there's nothing to eat. _____
4. In the trees, he finds fruit to eat. _____
5. The tea he makes has a lot of orange juice. _____

AFTER YOU WATCH

4 Work with a partner. Imagine that there is a fire in your home. You must leave in five minutes. What three things would you take with you?

> I'd definitely take my cat. And my phone . . . and my iPad!

82 | Unit 6

The START OF THE WEB

Unit 6 Video 6.3

BEFORE YOU WATCH

1 Write sentences using at least three of the words below.

| cell phone | message | network | text | web | wireless |

1. _____
2. _____
3. _____

WHILE YOU WATCH

2 Watch the video. Answer the questions.

1. In the early days, where did most people use the Internet? _____
2. What did computers look like in the 1960s? _____
3. Who used computers in the 1960s? _____
4. When was the first email sent? _____
5. How did computers change in the 1980s and 1990s? _____

3 Watch the video again. Are the sentences true (*T*) or false (*F*)? Correct the false sentences.

1. Computers have always communicated with each other. _____
2. ARPANET was one of the first computer networks. _____
3. Computer networks have become smaller and cheaper. _____
4. Web pages and chat rooms became popular in the 1960s. _____
5. We can expect the Internet to continue growing. _____

AFTER YOU WATCH

4 Work in small groups. Complete the chart. Discuss: What websites did you like two years ago? What websites do you like now?

Websites I liked two years ago	Websites I like now
Facebook	*Tumblr*

Unit 6 | 83

Let's CELEBRATE

Unit 7 Video 7.1

BEFORE YOU WATCH

1 Look at the picture from the video. Answer the question.

This is a celebration in China. What festivals or holidays do people celebrate with fireworks in your country?

_____

WHILE YOU WATCH

2 Watch the video. Complete the phrases with the name of the correct country, then match them with phrases a–d to make true sentences.

1. People in ____China____ celebrate New Year's by ____
2. In winter, many people in _____ like to ____
3. In _____, spring is a time for ____
4. Autumn in _____ is when people celebrate ____

a. swim in outdoor pools.
b. Diwali.
c. watching cherry blossoms and picnicking.
d. lighting fireworks.

3 Watch the video again. Complete the sentences with the words you hear.

1. People all over the world enjoy celebrating the changing _____.
2. In China, _____ marks the beginning of a _____.
3. It's a time for visiting _____ and _____.
4. In Japan, _____ is the time of renewal.
5. In India, it's Diwali – the festival of _____ and the beginning of a _____ year.

AFTER YOU WATCH

4 Work in small groups. Discuss: How do you mark the changing of seasons? Do you wear different clothes, eat different foods, or do different things in each season?

> In the summer, I wear shorts and T-shirts and I go swimming almost every day. In the winter, I stay inside!

84 | Unit 7

Like FATHER, LIKE DAUGHTER

Unit 7 Video 7.3

BEFORE YOU WATCH

1 Look at the picture from the video. Answer the questions.

What is this person doing? Where do you think he is? _____

WHILE YOU WATCH

2 Watch the video. Circle the correct words to complete the sentences.

1. The first cliff divers were **fishermen / boaters**.
2. For nearly **88 / 80** years, only men were cliff divers.
3. José Luis is called "The Knife" because his dives are so **strong / precise**.
4. Iris's mother says that **diving / school** is first.
5. Before she dives, Iris feels **nervous / peaceful**.

3 Watch the video again. Answer the questions.

1. What is Acapulco famous for? _____
2. What did the fishermen challenge each other to do? _____
3. What tradition is Iris ready to change? _____
4. When does Iris practice diving? _____
5. How high is Iris's dive today? _____

AFTER YOU WATCH

4 Work with a partner. Discuss: What sports used to be only for men, but now are for women, too? What sports still do not include women?

> Soccer and basketball used to be only for men. I don't think there are any women playing football ...

A LOST CIVILIZATION

Unit 8 Video 8.1

BEFORE YOU WATCH

1 Look at the pictures from the video and read the definitions. Complete the sentences with the correct words.

1. A worker removes a body from a _____ in the desert.

2. This _____ had been _____ for more than 700 years.

3. They found _____ such as this gold pitcher in the graves.

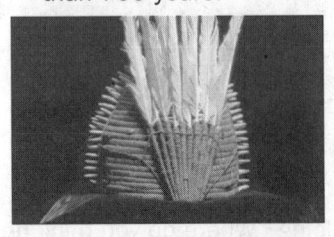

4. Some of the hats they found had the feathers of _____ birds.

artifacts: objects that were made by people long ago
grave: a place where a dead person is buried
mummy: a dead body that has been preserved
preserved: kept from decay; kept in its original condition
tropical: from the tropics (the hottest area on Earth)

WHILE YOU WATCH

2 Watch the video. Circle the correct words.

1. The Atacama Desert is next to the **Atlantic / Pacific** Ocean.
2. The bodies were preserved by the dry, **salty / heavy** sand.
3. Today there are **a few / no** buildings in the area.
4. Many graves had one or two **human / animal** heads.
5. The Amazon Forest is **near / far from** the Atacama Desert.

3 Watch the video again. Answer the questions.

1. What did workers discover in Peru about 15 years ago? _____
2. When did the Chiribaya live in the Ilo Valley? _____
3. How many people probably lived there? _____
4. Where did they get wool for their clothes? _____
5. Where might the tropical feathers have come from? _____

AFTER YOU WATCH

4 What do you think life was like where you live 2,000 years ago? How many people lived there? What animals and plants lived there? Draw a picture, and then describe it to a partner.

> So, 2,000 ago, about 1,000 people lived here. There were rabbits and bears and chickens. There were more trees and plants.

Mysteries OF THE BRAIN

Unit 8 Video 8.3

BEFORE YOU WATCH

1 Look at this picture from the video. Do you think the statements are true (*T*) or false (*F*)?

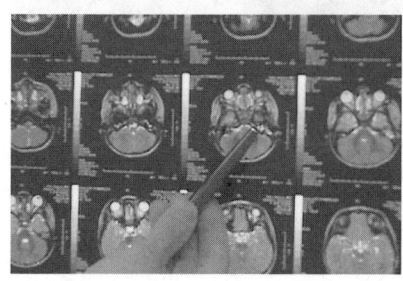

1. Scientists now understand how the brain works. _____
2. When something goes wrong with the brain, scientists can predict what will happen. _____
3. Each part of your brain has a different job. _____

WHILE YOU WATCH

2 Watch the video. Match the phrases to make true sentences.

1. When Michael was 10, he _____
2. A few years later, scientists _____
3. They found that not all parts of his brain _____
4. Dr. Jill Taylor's brain _____
5. After she was in the hospital, Jill _____

a. was damaged.
b. became interested in art.
c. were advanced.
d. graduated from college.
e. studied his brain.

3 Watch the video again. Correct the mistake in the sentences.

1. We can do amazing things when our mind and ~~hands~~ *body* work together. _____
2. Michael does very well answering the doctors' questions about words and faces. _____
3. We know that the same parts of the brain control how we think and feel. _____
4. Dr. Jill Bolte Taylor was doing research on the human body. _____
5. We don't have many unanswered questions about the brain. _____

AFTER YOU WATCH

4 Work with a small group. Think about the different ways of learning. How do you prefer to learn something – by seeing, hearing, or doing?

> I like learning by seeing. I can remember things better if I can visualize the image in a book or the word on a page.

On THE RUN

Unit 9 Video 9.1

BEFORE YOU WATCH

1 Look at these pictures from the video. Circle the correct answers.

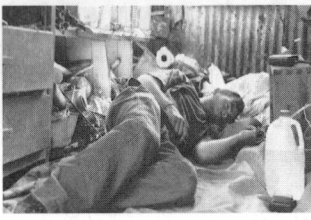

1. This man probably lives _____.
   a. with his family
   b. by himself
   c. with his friends

2. He probably _____.
   a. works in an office
   b. goes to school
   c. neither a. or b.

3. He probably has _____.
   a. cheated on a test
   b. done something illegal
   c. lied to his friend

WHILE YOU WATCH

2 Watch the video. Match the phrases to make true sentences.

1. First, Jamey stole _____
2. Then, he stole _____
3. When he was 18, he began stealing _____
4. Then, he hid from the _____

a. cars.
b. police.
c. chickens.
d. a horse.

3 Watch the video again. Answer the questions.

1. When did Jamey's crimes begin? _____
2. What did his best friend say about Jamey's actions? _____
3. Where did Jamey hide after he stole a car? _____
4. What did his mother tell him to do? _____
5. Where did the police find Jamey? _____
6. Where is Jamey now? _____

AFTER YOU WATCH

4 Complete this chart about Jamey. Then work with a partner. Compare what you wrote. Did you see and hear the same things?

Physical description	
What he thinks / says	
What he does	
What other people say about him	

Insectmobile

Unit 9 Video 9.3

BEFORE YOU WATCH

1 Look at the picture from the video. Answer the questions.

What do you think this object is? What is its function? _____

_____

WHILE YOU WATCH

2 Watch the video. Match the phrases to make true sentences.

1. The scientists get a flat tire and they _____
2. To learn more about insects, they _____
3. They learn that insects with six legs _____
4. Then, they _____
5. Finally, they _____

a. are really stable.
b. build a prototype.
c. test the real vehicle.
d. decide that legs may be better than wheels.
e. go to a university to talk to an expert.

3 Watch the video again. Circle the correct adverbs.

1. The scientists are driving when **finally / suddenly** they get a flat tire.
2. The broken wheel **actually / really** gives them some new ideas.
3. They decide that **clearly / slightly** there's a reason creatures have legs instead of wheels.
4. **Fortunately / Unfortunately**, they find an expert on insects at the university.
5. **Finally / Suddenly**, they build a vehicle and test it.

AFTER YOU WATCH

4 Work with a small group. Discuss: How would you improve an object you use every day, such as your phone or your car?

> Well, I'd make my phone do everything my computer can do. I'd make my car respond to voice commands. I'd also make the seats more comfortable.

Future DIRECTIONS

Unit 10 Video 10.1

BEFORE YOU WATCH

1 **Look at these pictures from the video. Answer the questions.**

1. What do you think this woman's job might be? _____

2. Like most people in China, she is an only child. How do you think being an only child affects her relationship with her parents? _____

WHILE YOU WATCH

2 **Watch the video. Answer the questions.**

1. How does Jolene start each day? _____

2. What does Jolene say about herself? _____

3. What are her two jobs? _____

4. What do her parents think of her career? _____

5. What does she sometimes worry about? _____

3 **Watch the video again. Match the columns to make phrases from the video.**

1. feel _____   a. as an equal
2. have _____   b. a different path in life
3. make _____   c. positive about
4. take _____   d. the guts to
5. treat _____   e. a contribution to

AFTER YOU WATCH

4 **Work in a small group. Make a list of at least three jobs that used to be done only by men or only by women, but are now done by both sexes. Why were these jobs done only by men or by women? Discuss your lists.**

> Well, soldiers used to be only men because it was a dangerous job. The leaders of many countries have usually been men, but today, it is more common for women to be in positions of power, too.

The Young and the BRAVE

Unit 10 Video 10.3

BEFORE YOU WATCH

1 Look at the pictures from the video. Answer the questions.

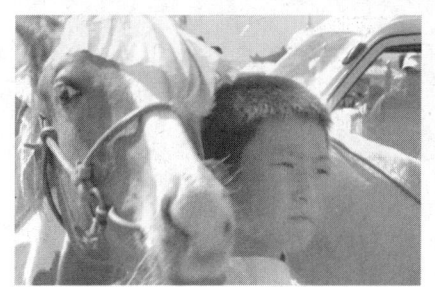

1. What do you think these children are doing and why? _____
2. What reward might they get for doing this? _____

WHILE YOU WATCH

2 Watch the video. Complete the sentences.

1. Inner Mongolia has thousands of kilometers of grasslands and _____.
2. They play the same games today that they played _____ ago.
3. The children had to train for the race for _____.
4. They ride their horses without _____.
5. When their horses get tired, the children _____ to them.

3 Watch the video again. Answer the questions.

1. What abilities are Mongols famous for? _____
2. When do many Mongol children learn how to ride horses? _____
3. How old are the children in the horse race? _____
4. How long is the race? _____
5. Who wins the race? _____

AFTER YOU WATCH

4 Work with a partner. Discuss: Are there certain things that children do better than adults? Why?

> Children are usually better with technology than adults are. I think children can learn things on a computer faster than adults because they're not afraid of technology.

This page intentionally left blank.

Irregular verbs

Base Verb	Simple Past	Past Participle
babysit	babysat	babysat
be	was, were	been
beat	beat	beat
become	became	become
begin	began	begun
bite	bit	bitten
bleed	bled	bled
blow	blew	blown
break	broke	broken
bring	brought	brought
build	built	built
burn	burned	burned/burnt
buy	bought	bought
catch	caught	caught
choose	chose	chosen
come	came	come
cost	cost	cost
cut	cut	cut
deal	dealt	dealt
dive	dived/dove	dived
do	did	done
draw	drew	drawn
dream	dreamed/dreamt	dreamed/dreamt
drink	drank	drunk
drive	drove	driven
eat	ate	eaten
fall	fell	fallen
feel	felt	felt
fight	fought	fought
find	found	found
fit	fit	fit
fly	flew	flown
forget	forgot	forgotten
freeze	froze	frozen
get	got	gotten
give	gave	given
go	went	gone
grow	grew	grown
hang	hung	hung
have	had	had
hear	heard	heard
hide	hid	hidden
hit	hit	hit
hold	held	held
hurt	hurt	hurt
keep	kept	kept
know	knew	known
lead	led	led

Base Verb	Simple Past	Past Participle
leave	left	left
let	let	let
lie	lay	lain
light	lit	lit
lose	lost	lost
make	made	made
mean	meant	meant
meet	met	met
pay	paid	paid
prove	proved	proven
put	put	put
quit	quit	quit
read	read	read
ride	rode	ridden
ring	rang	rung
rise	rose	risen
run	ran	run
say	said	said
see	saw	seen
sell	sold	sold
send	sent	sent
set	set	set
shoot	shot	shot
show	showed	shown
shut	shut	shut
sing	sang	sung
sink	sank	sunk
sit	sat	sat
sleep	slept	slept
speak	spoke	spoken
spend	spent	spent
spread	spread	spread
stand	stood	stood
steal	stole	stolen
stick	stuck	stuck
strike	struck	struck/stricken
swim	swam	swum
take	took	taken
teach	taught	taught
tell	told	told
think	thought	thought
throw	threw	thrown
understand	understood	understood
wake	woke	woken
wear	wore	worn
win	won	won
write	wrote	written

Credits

The authors and publishers acknowledge the following sources of copyright material and are grateful for the permissions granted. While every effort has been made, it has not always been possible to identify the sources of all the material used, or to trace all copyright holders. If any omissions are brought to our notice, we will be happy to include the appropriate acknowledgements on reprinting.

p. 2-3 (B/G): Getty Images/Ian McKinnell; p. 3 (1): Shutterstock Images/RossHelen; p. 3 (2): Shutterstock Images/enciktat; p. 3 (3): Alamy/©Tatiana Morozova; p. 3 (4): Shutterstock Images/Fotogenix; p. 3 (5): Corbis/W2 Photography; p. 4 (L): Getty Images/murat sarica; p. 4 (B/G): Shutterstock Images/Pixsooz; p. 5 (R): Shutterstock Images/marekuliasz; p. 6 (TL): Alamy/©ClassicStock; p. 6 (TCL): Shutterstock Images/Hector Sanchez; p. 6 (BCL): Shutterstock Images/Filip Fuxa; p. 6 (TBL): Alamy/©trekkerimages; p. 6 (BL): Getty Images/TimZillion; p. 7 (R): Shutterstock Images/CroMary; p. 8 (BL): Getty Images/Julia Fishkin; p. 8 (BR): Getty Images/Denis O'Regan; p. 9 (TL): Getty Images/T.J. Kirkpatrick; p. 10 (TL): Getty Images/Charles Gullung; p. 10 (CL): Alamy/©Frances Roberts; p. 10 (C): Alamy/©moodboard; p. 10 (B/G): Shutterstock Images/nikkytok; p. 12 (B/G): Alamy/©Stock Foundry Images; p. 13 (a): Getty Images/Aminart; p. 13 (b): Alamy/©Hero Images Inc.; p. 13 (c): Getty Images/DragonImages; p. 13 (d): Alamy/©STOCK4B GmbH; p. 13 (e): Alamy/©Bob Ebbesen; p. 14 (L): Darío Rodríguez/DESNIVEL./Courtesy of Robyn Raboutou; p. 15 (R): Getty Images/zhekos; p. 16 (TL): Getty Images/Tetra Images; p. 17 (L): Shutterstock Images/traithep khampitoon; p. 18 (TL): Alamy/©PhotoAlto; p. 18 (BL): Shutterstock Images/Oleg Vinnichenko; p. 19 (TR): Getty Images/sturti; p. 20 (CR): Getty Images/Dimitri Otis; p. 20 (TR, B/G): Alamy/©Sabena Jane Blackbird; p. 20 (TL): Alamy/©Greenshoots Communications; p. 22 (B/G): Alamy/©Michael Doolittle; p. 23 (a): Shutterstock Images/koosen; p. 23 (b): Alamy/©David Askham; p. 23 (c): Alamy/©imageBROKER; p. 23 (d): Alamy/©Jochen Tack; p. 23 (e): Getty Images/Ken Reid; p. 23 (BR): Shutterstock Images/PT Images; p. 24 (TL): Shutterstock Images/Ahturner; p. 24 (CL): NASA; p. 24 (BL): NASA; p. 24 (B/G): Shutterstock Images/JaySi; p. 25 (R): Alamy/©Kevin Galvin; p. 26 (TL): Alamy/©GARY DOAK; p. 26 (a): Shutterstock Images/Elnur; p. 26 (b): Getty Images/Kali Nine LLC; p. 26 (c): Alamy/©Kip Evans; p. 26 (d): Shutterstock Images/Amble Design; p. 26 (e): Shutterstock Images/Volt Collection; p. 26 (f): Getty Images/Anatoliy Babiy; p. 26 (g): Alamy/©ZUMA Press, Inc.; p. 26 (h): Shutterstock Images/Stephen Coburn; p. 28 (TL): Getty Images/Jamie Grill; p. 28 (CL): Shutterstock Images/Nadiia Korol; p. 28 (BL): Shutterstock Images/cocoo; p. 29 (TL): Shutterstock Images/Goodluz; p. 30 (TL): Getty Images/Niklas Halle'n/Barcroft India/Barcroft Media; p. 30 (CR): Sascha Baumann/Getty Images; p. 30 (TR, B/G): Shutterstock Images/Evgeny Karandaev; p. 32 (B/G): Getty Images/Hemant Mehta; p. 33 (1): Shutterstock Images/Andrey Armyagov; p. 33 (2): Getty Images/Peter Johansky; p. 33 (3): Shutterstock Images/Joe Belanger; p. 33 (4): Alamy/©Studio51; p. 33 (5): Shutterstock Images/L. Kragt Bakker; p. 33 (5): Shutterstock Images/Sheila_Fitzgerald; p. 33 (6): Shutterstock Images/Masson; p. 33 (7): Alamy/©Profimedia.CZ a.s.; p. 33 (8): Alamy/©Studio51; p. 33 (9): Shutterstock Images/Catalin Petolea; p. 34 (TL): Shutterstock Images/Nomad_Soul; p. 34 (TR): YOSHIKAZU TSUNO/AFP/GettyImages; p. 34 (BL): Shutterstock Images/SAAC; p. 34 (BR): Shutterstock Images/M. Unal Ozmen; p. 36 (TL): Getty Images/Andy Reynolds; p. 36 (a): Getty Images/C_yung; p. 36 (b): Shutterstock Images/Isantilli; p. 36 (c): Getty Images/Dennis Gottlieb; p. 36 (d): Getty Images/Kate Baldwin; p. 36 (e): Shutterstock Images/Chad Zuber; p. 36 (f): Getty Images/Nicole S. Young; p. 37 (R): Shutterstock Images/Alexeysun; p. 38 (TL): Shutterstock Images/Robnroll; p. 38 (TR): Alamy/©Bon Appetit; p. 39 (TR): Shutterstock Images/Joe Gough; p. 40 (B/G): Shutterstock Images/wavebreakmedia; p. 40 (TL): Shutterstock Images/kai keisuke; p. 40 (CL): Shutterstock Images/pictafolio; p. 40 (TC): Getty Images/Arnold H. Drapkin; p. 40 (TL): Alamy/©Mahdees Mahjoob; p. 40 (CR): Alamy/©Mode Images; p. 42 (B/G): Getty Images/Peter Dazeley; p. 44 (TL): Getty Images/L.Cohen/WireImage/Nordstrom; p. 44 (CL): Getty Images/STEPHANE DE SAKUTIN/AFP; p. 44 (BL): Getty Images/Harry How; p. 45 (R): Alamy/©lemonade; p. 46 (TL): Getty Images/urfinguss; p. 46 (BL): Shutterstock Images/cromic; p. 48 (TL): Alamy/©ALAN EDWARDS; p. 48 (CL): Getty Images/Logan Fazio/FilmMagic; p. 48 (BL): Getty Images/Peter Kramer/NBC/NBC NewsWire; p. 49 (R): Markus Mainka/Shutterstock; p. 49 (TL): Steve Collender/Shutterstock; p. 49 (TR): Shutterstock Images/joycedragan; p. 50 (TR): Getty Images/Peter Dazeley; p. 50 (C): Getty Images/Brad Barket; p. 50 (BR): Shutterstock Images/Helga Esteb; p. 50 (B/G): Shutterstock Images/Apples Eyes Studio; p. 52 (B/G): Getty Images/Kevin Elvis King; p. 54 (B/G): Alamy/©Peter M. Wilson; p. 55 (1): Shutterstock Images/Michael Dechev; p. 55 (2): Shutterstock Images/Sanit Fuangnakhon; p. 55 (3): Shutterstock Images/Filip Bjorkman; p. 55 (4): Shutterstock Images/Cynoclub; p. 55 (5): Shutterstock Images/Chimpinski; p. 55 (6): Shutterstock Images/Olga Popova; p. 55 (7): Shutterstock Images/Minerva Studio; p. 55 (8): Shutterstock Images/Darren Pullman; p. 55 (9): Getty Images/Pulse/Fuse; p. 55 (10): Shutterstock Images/Ivaschenko Roman; p. 56 (L): Corbis/©ROLEX DELA PENA/epa; p. 56 (R): Corbis/©DIVYAKANT SOLANKI/epa; p. 58 (TL): Alamy/©Idealink Photography; p. 59 (R): Getty Images/toddmedia; p. 60 (TL): Alamy/©B.O'Kane; p. 61 (TL): Shutterstock Images/fotoslaz; p. 61 (TL): Shutterstock Images/Olga Knutova; p. 62 (L): Alamy/©The Art Archive; p. 62 (L): Alamy/©Francesco Gustincich; p. 62 (CR): Corbis/©NingJie; p. 62 (R): Shutterstock Images/Igor Kovalchuk; p. 62 (B/G): Shutterstock Images/Fedor Selivanov; p. 64 (B/G) Corbis/ROBIN UTRECHT FOTOGRAFIE/HillCreek Pictures; p. 65 (1): Getty Images/Jupiterimages; p. 65 (2): Getty Images/ERproductions Ltd; p. 65 (3): Alamy/©Tony Watson; p. 65 (4): Shutterstock Images/Taras Vyshnya; p. 65 (5): Getty Images/Image Source; p. 65 (6): Alamy/©Blue Jean Images; p. 65 (7): Shutterstock Images/Richard Thornton; p. 65 (8): Alamy/©Datacraft - QxQ images; p. 65 (9): Corbis/Roger Brooks; p. 66 (T): Shutterstock Images/gualtiero boffi; p. 66 (TR): Corbis/Jon-Michael Sullivan/Staff; p. 66 (L): Shutterstock Images/HomeStudio; p. 66 (BR): Shutterstock Images/Mike Degteariov; p. 67 (R): Getty Images/mediaphotos; p. 67 (CR): Shutterstock Images/Dan Kosmayer; p. 68 (L): Shutterstock Images/topten22photo; p. 68 (TCL): Alamy/©FocusChina; p. 68 (BCL): Shutterstock Images/Paolo Bona; p. 68 (BL): Alamy/©ZUMA Press, Inc.; p. 69 (R): Alamy/©Rob Crandall; p. 70 (L): Alamy/©ImagesBazaar; p. 71 (TR): Alamy/©Corbis Super RF; p. 72 (TR): Getty Images/Chung Sung-Jun; p. 72 (T): Getty Images/Chung Sung-Jun; p. 72 (C): Shutterstock Images/Soultkd; p. 72 (B/G): Shutterstock Images/leungchopan; p. 74 (B/G): Getty Images/Borut Furlan; p. 76 (TL): Getty Images/New York Daily News Archive/contributor; p. 76 (CL): Alamy/©Randy Duchaine; p. 76 (R): Getty Images/Maremagnum; p. 77 (L): Shutterstock Images/MichaelTaylor; p. 78 (T): Getty Images/Joseph Devenney; p. 78 (BL): Getty Images/Carol Yepes; p. 80 (CL): Alamy/©Ingram Publishing; p. 80 (BL): Alamy/©Nature Picture Library; p. 81 (TL): Shutterstock Images/cenap refik ongan; p. 81 (CL): Shutterstock Images/NorGal; p. 81 (TR): Getty Images/Thinkstock/Sini?a Bota?; p. 82 (TR, B/G): Image courtesy of the Beinecke Library; p. 82 (L): Image courtesy of the Beinecke Library; p. 84 (B/G): Getty Images/John Lund; p. 85 (L): Alamy/©Everett Collection Inc; p. 85 (BL): Alamy/©Studio Works; p. 85 (BC): Alamy/©Ben Molyneux; p. 85 (BR): Corbis/©Bettmann; p. 86 (T): Shutterstock Images/MaxyM; p. 86 (L): Shutterstock Images/Emilio100; p. 87 (R): Shutterstock Images/M. Unal Ozmen; p. 88 (L): Shutterstock Images/Soumitra Pendse; p. 89 (1): Getty Images/Cavan Images; p. 89 (2): Shutterstock Images/Kingarion; p. 89 (3): Alamy/©Trinity Mirror/Mirrorpix; p. 90 (TL): Corbis/©Bettmann; p. 91 (TR): Shutterstock Images/Stacy Barnett; p. 92 (T): Shutterstock Images/MaraZe; p. 92 (T): Shutterstock Images/kravka;p. 92 (T): Getty Images/Witold Skrypczak; p. 92 (C): Alamy/©Emily Riddell; p. 92 (CR): Getty Images/traveler1116; p. 92 (B/G): Shutterstock Images/Aivoges; p. 92 (TL): Shutterstock Images/Kravka; p. 94 (B/G): Corbis/©Juice Images; p. 95 (T): Shutterstock Images/Air Images; p. 95 (TR): Shutterstock Images/wavebreakmedia; p. 95 (CR): Alamy/©Jeff Morgan 16; p. 95 (BR): Getty Images/moodboard; p. 96 (TL): Alamy/©Juice Images; p. 96 (CL): Shutterstock Images/Peter Gudella; p. 96 (BL): Shutterstock Images/donatas1205; p. 97 (B): Alamy/©B Christopher; p. 98 (T): Shutterstock Images/Africa Studio; p. 98 (1): Shutterstock Images/Africa Studio; p. 98 (2): Shutterstock Images/racorn; p. 98 (3): Getty Images/VikZa; p. 98 (4): Getty Images/Jetta Productions; p. 98 (5): Shutterstock Images/Izf; p. 98 (6): Getty Images/Digital Vision.; p. 98 (7): Alamy/©David Young-Wolff; p. 98 (8): Shutterstock Images/Sasha Samardzija; p. 98 (9): Alamy/©Ira Berger; p. 98 (BL): Alamy/©GraficallyMinded; p. 99 (L): Getty Images/Cultura/Leon Harris; p. 100 (TL): Shutterstock Images/Jultud; p. 100 (TCL): Shutterstock Images/Fetullah Mercan; p. 100 (CL): Shutterstock Images/Nightscorp; p. 100 (BCL): Getty Images/Charles Mann; p. 100 (BL): Shutterstock Images/Everything; p. 101 (TL): Alamy/©dpa picture alliance archive; p. 102 (TL): Getty Images/Pamela Martin; p. 102 (CL): Getty Images/Brendon Thorne; p. 102 (BL): Shutterstock Images/Al Bello; p. 102 (B/G): Shutterstock Images/Marish; p. 104 (B/G): Corbis/©Arctic-Images; p. 119 (TR): Shutterstock Images/Lucy; p. 119 (CR): Shutterstock Images/American Spirit; p. 120 (BR): Shutterstock Images/wandee007; Back cover: Shutterstock Images/Cbenjasuwan.

Front cover photography by Alamy/©Image Source Plus.

The publishers are grateful to the following illustrators:
Anni Betts: p. 50, 86, 99; Q2A Media Services, Inc.: p. 27, 43, 58, 73, 75, 116, 117, 118, 120.

All video stills by kind permission of:
Discovery Communications, LLC 2015: p. 2 (1, 3), 5, 10, 12 (1, 3, 4), 15, 20, 21, 22 (1, 3), 25, 30, 32 (1, 3, 4), 35, 40, 41, 42 (1, 3), 45, 50, 54 (1, 3, 4), 57, 62, 63, 64 (1, 3), 67, 72, 74 (1, 3, 4), 77, 82, 83, 84 (1, 3), 87, 92, 94 (1, 3, 4), 97, 102, 103, 116, 117, 118, 119, 120; Cambridge University Press: p. 2 (2), 8, 12 (2), 18, 22 (2), 28, 32 (2), 38, 42 (2), 48, 54 (2), 60, 63 (2), 70, 74 (2), 80, 84 (2), 90, 94 (2), 100.

Credits

The authors and publishers acknowledge the following sources of copyright material and are grateful for the permissions granted. While every effort has been made, it has not always been possible to identify the sources of all the material used, or to trace all copyright holders. If any omissions are brought to our notice, we will be happy to include the appropriate acknowledgements on reprinting.

p. 5 (BL): Alamy/©Jan Wlodarczyk; p. 7 (CL): Getty Images/Henrik Sorensen; p. 9 (BL): Getty Images/Zoranm; p. 15 (TL): Shutterstock/Testing; p. 16 (TL): Shutterstock/CandyBox Images; p. 17 (CL): Getty Images/M-imagephotography/iStockphoto; p. 18 (A): Getty Images/Hero Images; p. 18 (B): Shuttertstock/Jianghaistudio; p. 18 (C): Shutterstock/Halfpoint; p. 18 (D): Getty Images/Joel Eichler; p. 18 (E): Getty Images/Mark Bowden; p. 18 (F): Alamy/©Hero Images Inc.; p. 18 (G): Shutterstock/William Perugini; p. 18 (H): Shutterstock/Bikeriderlondon; p. 21 (CR): Shutterstock/Sean Locke Photography; p. 22 (1): Shutterstock/Yuriy Rudyy; p. 22 (2): Shutterstock/Photographee.eu; p. 22 (3): Shutterstock/Sergey Ryzhov; p. 22 (4): Shutterstock/Iakov Filimonov; p. 22 (5): Shutterstock/Photographee.eu; p. 22 (6): Shutterstock/ffolas; p. 22 (7): Shutterstock/Africa Studio; p. 22 (8): Getty Images/Ryerson Clark; p. 22 (9): Getty Images/Dennis Hoyne; p. 23 (TR): Shutterstock/Jacek Chabraszewski; p. 27 (CR): Shutterstock/Ulga; p. 30 (CL): Getty Images/PhotoAlto/Frederic Cirou; p. 31 (CL): Shutterstock/Konrad Mostert; p. 35 (C): Getty Images/DreamPictures; p. 36 (1): Shutterstock/Nickolay Khoroshkov; p. 36 (2): Shutterstock/R. MACKAY PHOTOGRAPHY, LLC; p. 36 (3): Shutterstock/Nikita Rogul; p. 36 (4): Getty Images/phanlop888/iStockphoto; p. 36 (5): Shutterstock/Maggee; p. 36 (6): Shutterstock/Africa Studio; p. 36 (7): Shutterstock/Mdblk1984; p. 36 (8): Shutterstock/Olga Kovalenko; p. 36 (9): Shutterstock/Olga Popova; p. 36 (10): Alamy/©Corbis Super; p. 41 (TR): Shutterstock/Igor Lateci; Shutterstock/sunlight77; p. 46 (CL): Shutterstock/PAUL ATKINSON; p. 47 (CR): Alamy/©Renato Granieri; p. 50 (TR): Alamy/©David Parker; p. 62 (CT): Getty Images/Andy Shaw/Bloomberg; p. 63 (CL): Alamy/©Paolo Patrizi; p. 69 (CR): Alamy/©ZUMA Press, Inc.; p. 70 (1): Alamy/©Gabe Palmer; p. 70 (2): Shutterstock/Valeriy Velikov; p. 70 (3): Getty Images/Steve Debenport; p. 70 (4): Shutterstock/Stasique; p. 70 (5): Alamy/©fStop Images GmbH; p. 70 (6): Shutterstock/Rido; p. 70 (7): Shutterstock/scyther5; p. 70 (8): Shutterstock/Andrey_Popov.

Front cover photography by Alamy/©Image Source Plus.

The publishers are grateful to the following illustrators:
Q2A Media Services, Inc.

All video stills by kind permission of Discovery Communications, LLC 2015.

Notes

Notes

Notes